Adventures of Fish & Game Wardens

Volume 5

Vermont Wild

Adventures of Fish & Game Wardens

Volume 5

Written by **Megan Price**

Cover by **Carrie Cook**

Illustrated by **Bob Lutz**

Pine Marten Press

Pine Marten Press

Charlotte, Vermont 05445

First edition

Cover by Carrie Cook Designs

Typesetting by Tyler Denis

Printed by L. Brown & Sons
Barre, Vermont

For information and book orders, visit our website:
www.PineMartenPress.com

ISBN: 978-0-9828872-2-6

Library of Congress Control Number: 2010934765

Answers to your most pressing questions:

Did the stories in this book really happen?
A deputy finds himself in a fight, his first hour on the job?
A poacher tries to wipe a warden out of his car?
An icy introduction to Lake Willoughby?
A raccoon seizure lands a warden in a pig sty?
Searching for clues in Lake Champlain?

Trust me, I ain't clever enough to make this stuff up!

Have some stories been embroidered just a little?
A whole lot less than, "The one that got away!"

What about the characters?
The wardens and deputy wardens are real.
Innocent bystanders names are used if they have a
sense of humor and swear they won't sue us.

What about the poachers?
We change their names and some of the particulars
so's not to further embarrass their families.
Their shenanigans and convictions are real!

Get ready, here it comes....

Big Legalese Disclaimer
Any resemblance to any individual,
living or dead, is one heck of a coincidence.

That's our story and we're sticking to it.

V

Dedication

*This book is dedicated to teachers who make
the difference in many
troubled kids' lives:
encouraging them to read,
believing in them,
and applauding their smallest success.*

*Special thanks to the following educators
who made a big difference in my life:*

**Sylvia Franklin Williams,
Peter Schoffstall,
Diane Jones Bardrof,
Valerie Zahn &
Dorothy Combs Hill**

Thank you for helping me find my way.

STORIES

"That's when I saw a big dark lump come looping around from the crowd of people behind Marc, headed straight for my deputy's head."

Deputy's First Day

Contributed by John Kapusta

I was casting about for a deputy and had interest from a young fellow named Marc Luneau. I knew his family and Marc had just graduated from Johnson State College, married his sweetheart and was about to start a teaching career.

Marc assured me he'd have the time to do both jobs and I had a good feeling about him. After getting through the preliminaries, I decided to give him a chance. We agreed he would join me a few days later, on a late summer afternoon.

I planned on driving over to some popular fishing spots and I'd show him how to check anglers' licenses – let him give it a try and break him in slowly. A lot of a warden's job is public relations. I wanted to see how Marc handled himself and how people responded to him.

My method for instructing new fellows was to have them ride along, keep their eyes open, follow my lead and ask me questions in private later. That's how most of us old school wardens had learned.

I had gotten Marc a uniform to wear. He was at least dressed for the part. But he had absolutely no training. I figured it was summer, it was daylight, this would be easy.

First on the agenda was the mundane task of filling the truck's gas tank. So, after I picked Marc up, we headed into downtown Hardwick.

I had just pulled into a filling station, shut the truck off and slid out the driver's door when an urgent call came over the truck's radio.

The Dispatcher said there was a brawl going on just up the street, outside the police station. Multiple people were involved. She asked for all available officers to respond.

When that kind of call comes in, it is "all hands on deck." Game wardens roll too.

I put the gas nozzle back in its stirrup, slapped the truck's tank cover shut, jumped back into the driver's seat and pulled my door shut. As I reached for my seatbelt, I turned my head towards Marc.

"Looks like you're about to meet another kind of wildlife," I grinned as I turned on the ignition and threw the shifter into Drive. "Hold on."

I made certain I wasn't going to hit any vehicles or people and sped off down the street, lights flashing.

We were the first ones with badges to arrive. There were no police at the station and it looked like the building was locked. The fracas was on the lawn.

As the truck rolled to the curb, I took a couple quick seconds to study the scene. I wanted an idea of who the aggressors were and if any weapons were involved.

There was a crowd. Sure enough, I saw adult males throwing windmill punches, yanking shirtsleeves and chasing one another about on the nicely mowed lawn.

A couple of fellows were pushing one another back and forth across the turf – heads bowed low. The tops of their heads almost touched.

Squint a little, imagine some antlers, and you'd swear they were bucks in the rut, slamming heads and shoulders trying to impress a doe.

There was a crowd of onlookers weaving in and out of the fray – women and teenagers and younger kids. It made it tough to tell just who was part of the brawl and who was just egging these guys on.

Maybe it was some of each?

I figured the onlookers were maybe family members or friends. My window was down and it was clear some of these folks had firm opinions and weren't shy in voicing them in loud, colorful language. It was almost like they were ringside and had money on the outcome.

"Just follow my lead," I said to Marc quietly before putting on my hat, jumping out of the truck and approaching the throng.

I tried a loud, "All right, Gentlemen. Now, let's calm down," as I waded in, hoping my hat and badge alone might be enough to get them to stop.

But this crew was beyond listening to a voice of reason.

The big guys were bouncing bellies against chests, standing nose to nose and shouting, then swinging their fists at one another. Smaller guys would run the periphery and when they spied an opening, run and jab somebody in the ribs or face, then dash to the outside again and hide.

"Hey, come on now. Calm down! It's over,"

I shouted as I stepped between two big, red faced fellows. I could see some swelling starting under one guy's eye and blood flowing from the other's nose.

I wanted to stop them from doing more damage to each other.

The crowd's calls for blood hadn't slowed just because we'd arrived. Some of them made it clear they didn't want us interfering in the dispute at all.

"Leave 'em alone! Get outta here! Let them settle it!" and similar derisive cheers resounded in my ears.

I had to keep my eyes open. Someone might just decide to take a poke at me.

Marc walked off to attempt to separate a knot of entwined humanity about 10 feet away, off to my right. All I could do was hope he kept himself safe.

I got the two big guys pulled apart and while they stood on either side of me, their heads down, their sides heaving while sucking air into their lungs like winded buffalo, I spoke calmly, trying to get them to settle down.

While their fists were open at their sides, I glanced

quickly over my shoulder to see if I could spot Marc.

There were kids and adults running all over.
I spotted the uniform and was pleased to see my
freshly minted deputy was on his feet. But he
appeared to have his hands full.

He was standing behind one of the pugilists, his
arms around the guy's belly, giving him a bear
hug – pinning the fellow's arms to his sides – to
keep him from swinging at another smaller guy
a few feet away.

It was unusual, but innovative and maybe smart.
No one would be hurt. I smiled. Behind Marc
were several onlookers, shouting and waving their
fists in the air.

I turned back to my fighters. I saw the look
change on one of their faces and sensed this guy
was about to fire up his fists again.

Sure enough, now that the pair had their wind
back, one of the fellows muttered something nasty
to the other one to get him stirred up.

A punch came flying, just missing my nose and
they were at it again.

I jumped back, waiting for a moment when I could
separate them again without becoming the third

man to be clobbered.

I took the opportunity to check on Marc's progress. Had his bear hug worked?

That's when I saw a big dark lump come looping around from the crowd of people in back of Marc, headed straight for my deputy's head.

I shouted, "Watch out, Marc!" But before I could even spit it all out, he was slammed in the side of the head by this thing that looked like a partially inflated football attached to a lighter colored hank of rope.

It was tough to see what had whumped my deputy trainee, because my view was continually shuttered by fellows lunging, swinging and stumbling around me like intoxicated adults on an Easter egg hunt.

But I'd seen enough to know my brand new assistant had been rocked by something the size of a pumpkin hitting him in the head. Was he hurt? Would he be able to stay on his feet? Who had done this?

I saw Marc release the fellow he was bear hugging.

The fellow stumbled forward a couple steps, turned a few degrees and walked away, looking back at my deputy with a funny look on his face. Maybe he was just happy he wasn't the one who got hit in the head.

I couldn't do anything about Marc. I had to get back to the fellows I was trying to get under control.

They separated and one started running away. I let the first man go by, then grabbed the forearm of the second, bigger man and spun him around, twisted his arm up behind his back and growled, "It's over."

Then I looked to my right again, trying to see if Marc was still standing or needed my help.

In addition to the adults, kids were running back and forth across the lawn like they were having a half court soccer match. Maybe they thought the adults were just playing?

I still didn't have the best view. But I managed to find Marc in about the same location and was happy to see he was still on his feet.

That was the good news.

But my jaw dropped when I saw him making another unorthodox fight move. Now, what was he up to?

The guy I had ahold of, he began to struggle a bit. "Calm down or you're going to jail," I told him.

But even as I was warning him, I again was looking over at Marc.

Just then, the fellow who had run off came charging back. He was intent on punching the man I was holding, or maybe both of us. It was hard to tell. But he was clearly planning to take some sort of cheap shot.

I stepped back and yanked the big man along with me, spun a quarter turn and when the smaller man brushed by, I stepped out and gave him a sharp elbow in the ribs with my free arm.

The attacker winced, doubled over, grabbed his side and his knees buckled. He hit the ground three feet away and slid on his forehead in the grass a foot, then rolled over.

I knew he wouldn't be up to fighting for at least a few seconds. He'd be trying to get his breath and hugging his aching ribs. If I was lucky, when he got back on his feet he'd decide to quit and slink away into the crowd.

"Let's go," I said to the fellow I was holding. I began marching him over to some shrubbery where I figured he'd be less likely to jump back into the fray.

That's when I saw my deputy reach up over his head with both arms, like he was about to take a high dive in the Olympics. Only there was a tangle of people around him.

"Holy smokes! What's he doing now?!!!" I asked myself. I stopped in my tracks and the big fellow in front of me skidded to a halt too.

This was not the kind of move you generally want to make in a bar fight, even if it is outdoors on the lawn. It leaves your face, your entire midsection, wide open to a punch.

I stood there mesmerized and more than a little concerned.

Marc bent his elbows, his hands disappeared behind his ears. His chin lowered to his chest.

"What in the world?" I asked myself. "Nah, he can't be..."

Out of the corner of my eye, I saw the mouth of the big man I was holding fall open and his eyes go wide. He was watching the man in the new uniform too. And he was just as curious.

Marc snapped at the waist like a mousetrap,

bending down hard and fast. He had ahold
of something behind him.

From out of the crowd, came a flash of yellow and
brown, arms and feet like a scarecrow flying.

What or whoever it was, flew over Marc's head
and back and landed with a thud on the ground
in front of him. They bounced once and then just
laid there, like a limp, steaming spaghetti noodle
dropped on the kitchen floor.

I was some impressed. I'd only ever seen that
kind of wrestling move on TV.

I congratulated myself for having hired such a
talented fellow and thought, "Nice move, Deputy!"

The big man next to me whispered, "Wow," and
reached up with his free hand to wipe a trickle of
blood still dripping from his nose.

We weren't the only ones impressed with Marc's
major league move.

I saw the expressions on the bystanders' faces
behind him immediately change. They went from
anger to shock in the blink of an eye. The shouting
stopped. They lowered their fists.

They went strangely silent.

It was odd.

I saw Marc look down at the ground in front of him. His eyes popped and his mouth opened into a huge, "Uh oh!"

There was a collective, "Oooooooh," on either side of Marc, like the chorus in a Greek play.

What was happening over there?

I pulled the fellow I was holding over to the edge of the lawn. "Stay here and don't move! Your fight's over," I told him. Then I ran over to see what was going on with Marc.

Someone was spread eagle on the ground in front of my deputy. I saw shoulder length blond hair, arms spread wide, one hand loosely holding a long, braided rope strap and three feet from that was a dark brown purse.

A purse? The kinda deflated football I saw was a purse?

It wasn't a guy Marc had flipped over his back and onto the ground, it was a woman, a young one. Worse, it was clear seeing her flat on her back, that she had a pronounced lump in the middle of her, under a billowing russet, ankle length skirt.

"Oh geez..." I sighed silently. "The poor guy's not an hour into the job and he's thrown a pregnant woman over his head. This is not good."

Kids stared at the lady on the ground and reached for their mother's hands.

Men who had been pounding on each other were surprised by the silence. They slowed, stood up straight, lowered their fists and began looking around.

One guy stopped right in the middle of his wind up. He looked over at the crowd and saw women holding hands to their faces in shock. When he spotted the blond flat on the ground, he realized something was seriously wrong.

The fighters chasing each other around the yard started to act like wind up toys with springs losing tension. The brawl slooooooowed to a stop.

Marc dropped to his knees and said, "Uh, Lady. Are you all right?"

Immediately, there was a crowd – one or two of the fighters among them – calling her name, checking her pulse, fanning her face – trying to be useful.

It was heartening to see Hardwick chivalry was

not dead. But this young lady was not having it.

She kicked her feet, waved her arms, sputtered and said, "Get away from me! Just give me a minute!"

She looked like she was trying to make a snow angel six months early. She was feisty, but I knew she was like a turned turtle. She wasn't going to be getting onto her feet without a little help, despite her big words.

I asked the crowd to, "Give her some air. Step back, please," and bent down to check her out.

"Are you hurting anywhere? Does your head hurt? Do you want us to call an ambulance and get you to a hospital?" I asked her.

"No! No! No!" she said, riling herself up more. "I just want everyone to leave me alone. I'll be fine."

I decided to try another angle in hopes of getting her to calm down.

"Is that your purse on the ground?" I asked her.

She gave me a dirty look and said, "Yes!" like I was asking her something obvious.

"Hunh," I said. "It looks an awful lot like what

I saw come out from behind my deputy a minute ago, hitting him hard in the side of his head."

She knew what I was implying. I saw her eyebrows shoot up and she suddenly stopped fuming and got quiet.

"And you say its yours?" I continued.

"Uh..." she said.

"You could be charged with assault, interfering with law enforcement and more," I said. "It is just downright dangerous what you did. Hitting someone from behind? Hitting anyone, period? What were you thinking?"

She turned her head away from me, stopped digging her heels into the ground and her eyes began to tear up.

I heard sirens coming at us from up the street and changed the subject.

"Are you certain you are all right? The baby too? Do you want a doctor to check you out?" I asked her one last time.

She raised her chin an inch, picked some grass off her skirt, sniffed and said, "I'm fine. Really. I just want to go home."

She raised her head to look Marc in the eye and said softly, "I'm sorry I hit you." A big tear ran down her cheek.

"Are you ready to get up then?" I asked her. She nodded.

"We'll help you to your feet. You just take it slow. If you feel woozy, you tell us," I said.

Marc took one elbow, I took the other and she got on her feet easily, then thanked us.

I gave her the purse, said, "Take care of that baby," and let her join her friends. I knew they would make certain she and the baby were all right.

When the police arrived, I walked over to tell them the fight appeared to be over with no real harm done. But maybe some of the people in the crowd would have another story and want to press charges. We had gotten there too late to see who threw the first punch.

In another 10 minutes, Marc and I were back in the truck and headed up the road, to a pond where he could check fishing licenses – like I'd planned.

We rolled along and didn't speak a word to one another for several minutes. I wanted Marc to literally get the situation behind him. I glanced over at him a time or two and saw his head was turned, looking out the passenger window. I figured he was wondering if this deputy warden job was really for him.

I was concerned this incident would prompt him to turn in his badge before he had really even started. I looked at my wristwatch and noted he'd been on the job a little more than an hour.

Before he got himself all twisted up, I turned towards him and asked cheerily, "Well, Marc, how do you like the job so far?" with some mischief in my voice.

Marc turned to look at me, his brows knitted together and asked innocently, "Is it always like this?"

I chuckled and shook my head. "Nah" I said, "You just got lucky!"

*"But by the time I got through half
the sandwich, my mouth felt like
I had chowed down on a tube
of window caulk."*

Snack Attack

Contributed by Walt Ackermann

Your stomach will tell you it's a long time between supper and breakfast when you are hidden in the woods on a cold night waiting for poachers to show up.

Working with Warden Ken Denton and fellow Deputy Warden Dave Stevenson, I came to be recognized as the fellow who carried food with me.

And I always brought enough to share.

But I wasn't the one driving to the store to buy meat and bread, lettuce and onions, the occasional tomato and mustard. I wasn't the one making the sandwiches or even wrapping them up, dropping them in a bag and tucking in a few cookies. I usually wasn't even the one filling my thermos with coffee.

It was my wife, Julie. She was the one keeping me fueled in every season and packing extra for the guys. And this, on top of making certain the kids had food at home.

Sometimes, I admit, I took what Julie did for granted. But she got my attention this particular evening and I've never, ever, forgotten it.

It was deer season, the middle of November. The days were short, the weather was cold and the hunters were serious. Add some guys who were desperate to get a big buck for bragging rights and you are looking at Vermont game wardens' busiest time of the year.

I had finished with my day job, grabbed some supper with Julie and the kids and was getting ready for night patrol.

The kids had put their dishes in the sink and run off into the living room to do their homework and turn on the TV. I got up to go change into my uniform and get ready for a frosty night, looking for poachers.

This night, Dave and I would be working together.

I went upstairs and reached into the closet for my uniform, grabbed a second pair of socks and got dressed.

When I came back into the kitchen, I found Julie up to her elbows in soapsuds. She'd gotten through the dishes and glasses. She was onto scrubbing the pots and pans she'd used to make dinner.

I looked around and didn't see the lunch bag
I always took with me.

I looked over at Julie as I pushed my feet into my
boots and prepared to lace them up.

"Where's my lunch? Come on. I gotta go. I'm
gonna be late," I nagged her.

She turned from the sink with a look that said,
"Are you kidding me? Do you know what kind of
day I've had? Can't you see how busy I am?" But
she didn't say a word.

At the same time I was talking to her, one of the
kids was calling, "Mom?" from the living room.

I didn't quit. I said, "Come on! I gotta get
going. I have to meet Dave. I'm late. Just
put something together."

"There isn't much in the house," Julie replied,
exasperated. "You said you'd stop at the grocery
store and pick up some things."

She was right. I had said that. But I'd been busy
too, and I just didn't stop and shop.

"You know I can eat anything," I said. "Just put

something together for tonight, will you? I gotta have something to eat."

Julie had worked all day too. And now she had to handle the kids alone, make certain they did their homework, took their baths and lay out clothes for them for the next morning. And if they didn't have clean clothes for school, maybe she'd be up late doing laundry too. She had to do all the stuff parents do for their kids, only without my help tonight.

I was headed off to be in the woods, like I'd been just about every night for more than a month, since late summer. And I'd been doing this for years. I loved being a deputy warden.

Julie scowled, pulled her arms out of the sink and reached for a dishtowel to dry her hands.

I ran back up the stairs to pick up something I'd forgotten. Looking back on it now, I realize I was a little snippy.

I could have been a whole lot nicer, a lot more appreciative. And I'm sure a lot of people would say I coulda just learned to make my own lunch.

But I didn't.

I came back downstairs a few minutes later and

there was a paper bag on the counter near the back door.

Julie was back over at the counter wiping pots dry and putting things away, finishing up.

"Is that it?" I said to her looking at the bag.

"Yes," she said. "There wasn't much to work with."

"All right, I'll catch you later," I said reaching for the bag and running out the door to my truck.

The plan was to head to Lunenberg where I would catch up with Dave. And that went okay. But looking for poachers isn't a desk job.

By the time we were ready for our middle of the night meal, Dave and I were sitting in his truck in back of a Cabot cemetery.

"I'm hungry," I said to Dave. "Let's see what Julie put together for us tonight."

I felt around the floorboards until my hand found the paper bag. I picked it up, opened it and pulled out one sandwich, then another.

"Here, Dave," I said. "Try this."

"You sure?" he said. "I don't want to take

your lunch."

I felt deeper into the bag. "Looks like she put three sandwiches in here. Of course, take one," I said. "I've got plenty."

I unwrapped my sandwich and bit into the white bread and got this funny taste in my mouth. It was thick, like mutton, but without any flavor. I thought I tasted some onions too. But I couldn't tell what else my wife had used for filling.

I was hungry, so I kept chewing. But I'd never had a sandwich that tasted like this one. It wasn't horrible, but it didn't taste like bologna or ham or turkey or roast beef or chicken.

I couldn't place the taste.

This is a job where you don't inspect your sandwich like you are conducting some sort of scientific experiment.

Our job was to be quiet, to not be seen or heard. You don't turn on the car's overhead light. You're given some food? Whatever it is, you just eat it and be thankful. It could be a long time until the next meal.

But by the time I got through half the sandwich, my mouth felt like I had chowed down on a tube of window caulk.

I stole a look sideways at Dave to see how he was doing with his sandwich.

Was he eating it?

My partner was slowly chewing along, looking straight ahead. He wasn't devouring it, but he wasn't grimacing either.

I remembered Julie had said we needed to get to the grocery store. I was thinking maybe Dave got something different, something better than I was eating, in his sandwich.

I hoped so anyhow.

I turned to Dave and said, "What'd you get?"

Maybe Dave could tell me what it was we were eating.

Dave stopped chewing.

He lowered the sandwich from his mouth and held it out a couple inches in front of him.

"I'm not sure," he said with a look of wonder on his face. It was so dark, we couldn't see anything but shadows.

I shook my head, shrugged my shoulders and
shoved the rest of my sandwich in my mouth.
I just wanted my stomach to stop gnawing at
me. Whatever it was, it would at least stop
the rumbling.

And Dave was eating his sandwich, right?
He wasn't complaining. But then I remembered
that Dave was a really polite guy, with good
manners. Give him pickled chicken brains and
he would thank you and eat it.

I swallowed the other half of my sandwich and
felt it slide down my throat and lie there like a
blob of glue.

For want of something else to do, I sat there trying
to place the taste.

"What in the world did Julie put between these
slices of bread?" I wondered.

Dave was behind me a couple bites. When he
finished, I said, "Hey, Dave, there's another
sandwich in here. You want it?"

"No thanks," he said, "I'm good. You go ahead."

Now, I noticed my tongue and the roof of my
mouth felt funny, like it was coated with wax
paper. I couldn't place the taste, but I didn't feel

quite right. I decided I had better skip eating a second sandwich too.

"Nah, I don't want it," I said to Dave. "If you change your mind, you take it. It's right here in the bag."

Dave nodded and said, "Okay. Thanks."

"Let me see if Julie put anything else in here for us," I said.

I dug beneath the third sandwich and felt something.

"Hey, there's a couple cookies here!" I said, "You want one with your coffee?"

"That would be good. Thank you," Dave said and he reached for his thermos while I leaned the other way and grabbed mine. The combination of the coffee and the cookie did a pretty good job of washing away whatever was in my sandwich. But I couldn't entirely shake the feeling I had window putty stuck between my teeth.

Dave and I stayed out on patrol until just before dawn. If poachers were busy, they had chosen well that night. We didn't hear or see anything.

I pulled into my driveway just as the sun was

streaming through the tops of the trees.

Julie was in the kitchen pretty much as I had left her. She was back at the sink. Only now, she was washing the breakfast dishes and our children were getting ready for the school bus.

I joked with the kids, talked with them briefly about how school was going. And once they were on the bus, I brought in my gear from the night before.

I dropped the paper bag on the counter, pulled a kitchen chair away from the table and sat down to take off my boots.

Julie walked over to the lunch bag and opened it.

"You didn't eat all your lunch," she said peering down into the bag. She said it in a strange way, like it was both a fact and a question.

"Nah," I said shaking my head and pulling hard at my boot heel.

I paused and looked up at her. "What was in those sandwiches anyhow? I don't know about the one Dave ate, but mine tasted pretty bad."

When you tell someone something they made was not good, they generally frown. They might even get defensive.

Instead, I saw a half smile come across my wife's lips. It was a "I know something you don't know" look.

I looked at her harder and tried again, "Did you do something different? They didn't taste like anything I'd had before."

"Oh" said Julie. "Really?"

"Yeah, mine just tasted really weird," I said, shaking my head. I could still taste it.

"I used what I could find," Julie replied, reaching for the refrigerator door. "There wasn't a lot in the house. We need groceries."

Something about the way she was talking. Her voice. She was acting kinda funny.

I stopped fiddling with my boots, put my foot down, leaned back and looked hard at her. I was trained to read people, to pick up on clues when something wasn't right.

And the way my wife was acting and speaking was strange.

I was seriously wondering, "What did she do?

What did Dave and I eat?"

Julie turned to face me and said, "Well, one of them was Crisco and onions. And the other was Crisco with mustard. And I think the sandwich you left in the bag – the third one – that may have had some chocolate syrup in with the Crisco."

My right hand flew to my stomach and my face went sour like I had swallowed a fly.

I tried to determine if there were stabbing pains rumbling down around inside me.

I felt a little tired, but who wouldn't after working day and night for weeks?

Julie stood looking at me. A smile came across her face and her eyes flashed like she was thinking of a joke.

"You said you could eat anything," she reminded me.

I got up and reached for the paper bag and took it gently from her. She didn't fight me. She just stood there watching with a crooked smile on her face, not saying a word.

I opened up the bag, lifted out the sandwich and opened it up slowly – like it was a firecracker

whose fuse had been touched off the night before
but never went BOOM.

What in the world had she fed us?

Or was she just kidding me?

I peeled the top piece of bread back a couple
inches and peered down at a layer that looked like
some glue colored mayonnaise with dark swirls.

I bent my head, took a sniff, then dipped my finger
into the mix, put it to my mouth and tasted it.

I made a face like a kid who just been spoon fed
their first brussel sprout by a parent they trusted
– who told them they'd loved 'em.

Julie couldn't contain herself any longer.

She started to laugh when I made a face like
a baby someone had fed a spoon of pureed kale.

"Gee whiz! Is that what Dave and I were eating last
night? It tastes awful," I said to her, grimacing.

"I told you there wasn't much to work with and
you said you could eat anything. So, I put
together what I could find," Julie said defiantly.

No wonder Dave decided he didn't want another

sandwich. No wonder my stomach agreed
with him.

I was speechless. And my mind raced forward.

What else had she done?

"Did you do anything to the coffee?" I asked her.

"No," Julie said, with a little shrug. "We had
plenty of coffee."

What was there to say?

I put the sandwich down, shook my head, walked
back across the kitchen, sat down and went back
to unlacing my boots.

But every once in awhile, when she thought I
wasn't looking, I stole a look at her and thought,
"What is going on with my wife? You trust
somebody completely and they do something like
this? Something way outta left field?"

Things changed after that.

From that day forward, when Julie told me on my
way out the door, "If you want me to make your
lunch, you need to stop at a store and pick up
whatever you want to eat," Brother, I listened.

I stopped pretending meat and bread and cookies

for our late night snacks just magically appeared in the fridge and transformed themselves into sandwiches and goodies, then jumped into a lunch bag for me to grab as I ran out the door.

Julie had made her point, without ever raising her voice.

Dave and I never again chowed down on a Crisco sandwich at 3 a.m.

Anyway, I'm pretty sure that's true.

*"Into the boat spilled 50 feet of net,
then 100 feet. And it just kept coming,
pulling me like a compass towards
the dock below the camp."*

Buoy Blab

Contributed by Denny Gaiotti

L ike solving puzzles?
Wardens do a lot of it.

A woman came up to me in a grocery
store, saying she wanted me to know there was
a fellow giving away fish. Not just one or two fish.
The story was the man was trying to give away
buckets of fresh fish.

Well, anyone can have a bit of luck now and
again and want to share the wealth. But there
are limits. And one fellow having that many fish
to give away, it certainly raised my suspicions.
I asked her for a name, a location, a description
of the fellow. But all she had was a rumor.

A few days later, I got a similar report, but from
a caller in a town miles away. He knew a little
more. He said the fellow had yellow perch, bass,
bluegills, bullhead, pike and more. But when I
asked for details, again, there weren't many to be
had. But he at least knew someone who might
know someone. So, I phoned them.

I found two people who said they had seen the man. One said he recalled sandy hair and a fellow in his thirties. Another person told me dark brown hair and a man in his forties. Neither had noticed the vehicle. It was seeing baskets of all these different kinds of fish that had stuck with them.

So, I figured there was some truth to the story and knew it was an adult male giving fish away, but that was it. In a rural area, where people know one another, that was odd. How come nobody could come up with a name or an address?

Worse for me, this generous fellow with all the fresh fish seemed to get around. One person saw him in a store parking lot offering fish to strangers. Another said they saw the guy doing the same thing, but 15 miles south.

I believed what people were telling me. But how was I going to find him?

Depending on the species, he could do a lot of damage to a fish population fast. And, of course, if this fellow was taking any fish illegally, it wasn't fair to everyone else who bought a license and was following the law. I decided I had to treat this like a big puzzle, which was what a lot of investigations were. Only with this case, I realized what I didn't know was just as important – maybe even more important – than what I did know.

I spread a map of my district on the kitchen table and tried to put what I had been told into information I could use. Of the several locations people reported seeing the fellow trying to give away fish, all three were in towns that bordered Lake Champlain.

And the kinds of fish people told me he was offering them? They were all species a fellow would find in the southern half of the lake. It seemed to me his catch was likely coming from below the Crown Point Bridge, connecting Vermont with New York.

I knew a lot of the fishermen who trolled the big lake's waters two or three times a week. I was certain if they had seen a fellow taking more than his share of fish, they would have definitely called to let me know.

They'd feel cheated.

The fact none of those fellows had called me to complain, told me they must not have seen him.

I didn't have time to stake out parking lots in hopes of spotting a man trying to give fish away. With the fellow never seeming to stick to one spot, that would be foolish. I had to make what little I did know work for me. If the fish were coming from Lake Champlain I decided that was where I needed to start.

It was a needle in a haystack kind of search, but
I was pretty certain Lake Champlain was at least
the right haystack – even if it is miles long and very
wet. Maybe, just maybe, I would spot something
or find someone that would bring me closer to the
fellow I needed to meet. But searching miles of
shoreline at night wouldn't work.

I needed daylight to look for clues.

And while there would be more people out on
the water and fishing on the weekend, I wasn't
looking for everybody. I figured it was a lot more
likely I was searching for one or two fellows with
something to hide. I decided to get out on the
water on a weekday, very early in the morning.

If an angler was doing something outside the
law on this scale, he'd be likely to have done his
fishing at night. He wouldn't want anyone to see
him. He'd have to hide, remove his lines, clean up
the site and move that catch all without anyone
seeing him. And that meant he'd probably want a
sliver of daylight, just with no one around.

He could fish at night with a headlamp, but
people staying at a camp, boating or night fishing
themselves might spot the glow and investigate.
He wouldn't want that.

I sensed this fellow was using early morning for
some part of his operation. And if I was going
to have any chance of finding him, that's when
I needed to be out on the water too. A weekday
would mean less people out on the lake. With
most people having to work, recreational boaters
would be few and far between in the middle of the
week, even in summer.

I hitched my boat to my truck before heading into
supper and made certain I had the truck's cab
pointed down the driveway onto the town road.
I wanted to be able to just climb behind the wheel,
a big mug of fresh hot coffee in my hand and head
out to the boat launch an hour before sunrise.

I climbed out of bed just before 3:30 a.m., got
dressed and with a cup of coffee in one hand and
my gear in the other, I walked out of the house
before the first bird chirped.

I landed at the fishing access with a few stars still
shining in the sky. No surprise, I was the only
person there.

I launched my 16 foot boat so early I startled a
family of mallards napping along the shoreline.
They skittered across the water, then settled back
down, happy I wasn't a fox.

The center of the lake was still covered in mist,

the water calm and there was no sign of life other than fish rising.

I wore a light jacket to keep the chill off me until the sun rose and warmed the day. I turned my boat lights on for safety, rowed about 250 feet out into the channel, then pulled the choke and started the outboard.

Once the engine warmed up, I headed North, slow, as if I was trolling. And I guess I was – just not for fish, but for a fisherman.

I studied the camps and docks along the Vermont shore, using my binoculars when I thought they might help me spot something.

It made sense to me whoever was catching all these fish was using a boat to haul them in. You'd have to be awful lucky and awful fast to reel in hundreds of fish with just a few fishing poles set up on shore. Even if just one man was seen attempting to give fish away, it could be two, three or more were involved.

Checking out camps with fishing boats tied in front of them was one of my interests this morning. Especially if I could get a look inside for the types of tackle they were carrying.

An open boat hull can provide a lot of clues.

When I saw fishing boats I would steer in a little closer and just casually look inside them as I rode by. Multiple fishing rods maybe set with grappling hooks, gaffs, maybe a net? Anything that would bring a lot of fish into a boat quickly would be worth my coming back and asking questions later.

I traveled for miles and while I spotted a dozen or more boats, I didn't see anything that would raise suspicion. And the only people I saw were a couple seated at a table behind a big picture window. They looked to be having breakfast. They stood and waved to me and raised their coffee cups as I drifted past.

I stopped now and again and listened for the sound of other boats on the water. If I got really lucky, I might catch somebody who had been fishing all night headed back to their camp. But there was no sound other than the occasional dog barking at me as I drifted by, turtles splashing into the lake when they felt I was too close and more ducks skittering across the water.

I knew it was early yet so I kept going. Other than dairy farmers, few people would be rolling out of bed before dawn. Maybe this fellow was so confident he wouldn't be caught he was taking care of business later?

You have to be an optimist in this business.

It was after 6 a.m. when I rounded a bend and saw a figure striding up the bank, away from the shoreline.

I saw a cabin sitting up on a knoll 60 feet away. He appeared to be headed there.

The fellow stopped in his tracks when he heard my motor. He glanced over his left shoulder, just long enough to see my boat and notice the uniform. He didn't smile or wave.

He turned his head back towards the camp and with his head down and elbows pumping, he did a sort of speed walk up to the camp. He opened the screen door, then a solid front door and went inside, shutting the front door so fast, the screen door bounced a few times before it settled.

I thought his behavior was kind of odd.

It was a beautiful summer morning. Most people would want to get a better look at the boat and its passenger coming down the lake. They'd turn to watch the bow split the water, sending the spray shimmering like diamonds.

They'd wave, maybe even shout out a greeting.

Like the couple in the camp a half hour earlier, it's polite to give someone a smile and a wave whether

you know them or not. Many people would even
motion you into the shore. They'd want to chat
about the weather, talk about the fishing or
ask about the wildlife you'd seen while out that
morning. Others would invite you to stretch your
legs, maybe have a cup of coffee with them.

But not this guy. He practically ran from me.

Did he just recall he'd left the coffee pot on?
Did he need to visit the bathroom? Or was he
hiding something?

I had a funny feeling it might be the latter, he
might be up to something.

I didn't crank up the engine, hit the shore hard,
leap out of my boat and go racing after him.
I knew where he was. I just kept drifting along
the lake, studying the place, looking at the yard
and noting a boat was tied to the dock.

I was like a slow torpedo – headed right for him,
but wanting to see if I could spot why he had
appeared to run when he saw a game warden.

This was farm country.

There was lots of elbow room between summer
cottages. And it wasn't unusual to see a group
of heifers enjoying the view from the million

dollar shoreline.

And that was the case here. His camp sat alone. There was a wooden dock about 24 feet long and a 12 foot, steel hulled rowboat tied there. If he was doing something illegal, he was pretty well hidden.

As I came parallel to the camp, maybe 400 feet from shore, I slowed the engine to a sputter and looked things over.

And that's when the sun touched on something gently bobbing in between my boat and the camp. It was low in the water and the color of mustard.

If it was litter, I wanted to pick it up. If it was marking something – what? I sat up a little straighter and aimed my bow towards the floater. When I came up alongside it, I cut the motor and reached over the gunwale and snagged it.

It was a faded plastic jug. And when I tugged on it, to get it out of the water, I found a nylon rope tied around the handle.

The jug wasn't litter. It was being used as a buoy. But what was it marking? No one would moor a boat so far out in this channel.

I looked for a name or some identification on the jug. Nothing.

I didn't want some boater to smack into this thing. The rope could wrap around a boat propeller and stop it dead, maybe even rip an outboard off a small boat. Someone could get hurt. This homemade buoy was a hazard.

I needed to get to the bottom of this find – literally. Hand over hand, I began to pull the rope out of the water and coil it on the floor of my boat. And as I tugged, the bow of my boat turned, like an Ouija board finder, pointing right towards the camp.

In about eight feet, the rope ended and I struck netting. It sported holes maybe three inches square.

I spread my legs to make room for whatever was going to come up with the net and took a breath. Then, hand over hand, I started hauling in whatever was hidden beneath the water.

It didn't take but a few seconds for the tug of fish on a line to run up into my hands. Fish were caught and struggling to free themselves.

Finding live fish stuck in the net told me it hadn't been set very long. It sounds odd, but fish can drown. And that's the fate of most fish who get caught in gill nets.

The nets are called that because they literally

grab fish by their gills, stopping them from going forward or back in the water. Unable to escape, fish drown because they cannot move their gills freely, which is key to their breathing.

I pulled and pulled and laid the netting in a loop in front of my feet, stopping to remove a flopping yellow perch or bass now and again. I dropped live fish over the back of my boat so they could swim away from the netting. Then I'd grab another handful of net.

It struck me whoever was doing this had chosen a great spot.

Thousands upon thousands of fish would swim through here. Maybe dozens of turtles, a few muskrats and diving ducks too. The net would not discriminate. It would catch anything that could not slip through the three inch holes, kill anything unlucky enough to swim into it.

And that's why gill nets were illegal.

After 25 feet or so of net, I realized I could be at this awhile. I shut off the boat motor, rolled up my sleeves, bent down and pulled at the netting with both hands.

Into the boat spilled 50 feet of net, then 100 feet. And it just kept coming, pulling me like a compass towards the dock below the camp.

I spent a good 15 minutes hauling in the knotted fabric, freeing struggling fish that were alive and piling the netting as neatly as I could onto the bottom of my boat. There was so much, it spilled over the seat in front of me and into the bow.

When I reached the end, I found myself at the camp dock. A rope was tied to one of the supports, hidden under the water a foot or two. I leaned back in my boat, reached for a knife in my pocket, opened it and cut the cord.

Now, I had the entire net – 300 feet – piled in front of me and spilling into the prow. I looked like a Louisiana shrimper.

I turned my attention to the 12 foot rowboat tied to the dock.

There was a wet tarp lying over a long, low mound in the center. I saw fins wave at me and heard a couple slaps smacking the aluminum hull.

The combination told me someone had hauled in that catch not long before I had rounded the bend. I had a good idea as to who that might be. It was time to visit the camp's occupants.

I tied up to the dock, stepped off and glanced up

at the cabin.

I saw a curtain move slightly, like someone had stuck an index finger behind a corner fold and peeked, then quickly let it fall. Maybe they didn't like the sight of me?

I pretended not to notice, stood up tall and walked up the grassy hill to the front door. I knocked on the screen door and waited. In a minute or so, a woman answered the door, wiping her hands on a dishtowel. I introduced myself and asked if anyone inside had been fishing recently.

"Oh. My husband fishes," she said with a smile. "He's in the back room."

"Would you please ask him to come out and speak with me?" I said.

She nodded and let the screen door fall shut. I heard a muted conversation inside the summer home. The fellow didn't rush out to meet me.

But in a couple minutes, he came to the door. I asked him to step outside and when he did, I introduced myself to him and asked him if he'd been fishing.

He said yes, pulled a wallet out of his back pocket and showed me his fishing license. It was the kind summer people get. He wasn't a Vermonter. But it was valid and I told him that he was good there.

He appeared a little nervous. He explained he was just renting the cottage for a few months. When I asked about the rowboat, he said it came with the camp and yes, he used it.

"Are those fish under the tarp in the rowboat ones you caught?" I asked him.

"Yes, I got them this morning," he said.

"With a gill net?" I asked him.

"Yeah," he shrugged, "that's the way we do it down home."

When I told him Vermont doesn't allow fish to be taken that way, he looked a little stunned.

"You can't do that here?" he asked incredulously. "It's legal where I come from."

That made me wonder if there were any fish left where he came from.

And while it might have been an interesting topic to discuss, I just stuck with enforcing Vermont law.

"Using a gill net isn't legal anywhere in Vermont,"

I said. I suggested he pick up a copy of Vermont's
fishing and hunting regulations, so he didn't
run into more trouble while spending his
summers here.

"Guess I should have read it before I started
fishing," he said with a sheepish grin. "I'm sorry.
I didn't know."

I told him his net would be coming with me along
with all the fish in his boat, since he had taken
them illegally. Both were evidence.

I handed him a citation for taking fish by illegal
means, told him he could contest the charge at
court or just pay the fine and urged him again to
read Vermont's fishing regulations. He nodded
and hung his head.

I walked down to his boat and lifted the tarp he'd
used to cover his haul before he'd scooted up into
the camp when he spotted me. It wasn't a pretty
sight. There were close to 300 fish there, all killed
by the net he had likely set the evening before.

I took his tarp and transferred the fish, one by
one, from his boat to mine. They, the net and the
tarp were all evidence now.

I backed my boat carefully out into the lake,
turned and headed back to the landing, a little

lower in the water than when I'd started out four hours earlier.

It was one of the biggest hauls I'd ever had the displeasure of confiscating.

If he'd continued to use the gill net, he might have done some real damage to fish populations in this part of the lake and probably killed a number of turtles, diving birds and mammals as well.

I'd followed my hunch, had some luck and managed to solve a tough puzzle. It was a good morning. And it taught me something.

When you're looking for a needle in a haystack in water, you need to think differently.

That needle you're chasing? It just may float.

*"I was ear deep in the pig pounded pudding
but refusing to let go of the catch pole.
I didn't want the raccoon to get away
after I'd come this far."*

ROCKY RESCUE

CONTRIBUTED BY JOHN KAPUSTA

The sun had been up about an hour on a steamy July morning when a fellow called me to say he knew of a family keeping a raccoon as a pet.

That was, and is, illegal. While most everyone agrees raccoons are cute as the dickens when little, they grow up fast. And mature raccoons have lousy dispositions, sharp claws and teeth they are not afraid to use. Add to this, they have tremendous strength for their size. Get in a disagreement with them and it's like trying to untangle screaming razor wire.

Odds were this raccoon was being fed dog or cat food and a bunch of treats – nothing like the diet the animal would have while foraging in the wild. Kept in a cage, apart from its kind and fed junk? No matter how you sliced it, it wasn't fair to the animal and it certainly wasn't safe for humans.

"Where's the raccoon kept on the property?" I asked the caller.

"He's in a big cage off to the left of the house as you pull into their driveway. They're homesteaders. They've got a little farm," I was told.

I thanked him for the tip and hung up the phone.

Wardens act fast when they get calls like this. People know they are not supposed to keep a wild animal as a pet. If they get wind the law is going to show up, many will take steps to keep the animal hidden. Sometimes they move it to the home of a family member or friend. If an animal is diseased, that means they just exposed more people to illness, even death.

I wanted to make this a priority and head right over there. But I had a problem.

My boss had scheduled a meeting for 1 p.m. in the district office, a two hour drive east of my house. This raccoon was an hour's drive away to the west.

Add up all the driving time and toss in a few minutes to get the raccoon and I would be cutting it awful close. Maybe too close.

My supervisor was a stickler for his wardens showing up on time, boots polished, our uniforms spotless and a fresh shave. Given how the job demanded we be out in the field, in all kinds of weather, tromping through mud and water, weaving through burdocks, thorn apples trees, oozing pine trees and every other kind of shrub that could tear or stick to our uniforms, it wasn't easy to meet his standards and actually do the job.

Unless, of course, you elected to just stay home, polish your boots and shave one more time before you headed out for his lengthy lectures.

The man loved to extol the virtues of deadly dull policies and procedures. We'd be trapped in a windowless conference room, where – regardless of the season – it was always hot enough to grow orchids. I dreaded his meetings.

I recognized there was a need to know this stuff, but to spend hours on it was too much for me.

I'd been late to meetings before and he'd made it clear he didn't like it. I always had good reasons – ones that involved doing my job. But it wouldn't matter if you said you stopped to rescue a baby from of a burning building.

We were like oil and water. And since he was my boss, I had to be careful. I knew if I showed up late to the meeting today, I'd be in real trouble.

I stood there a couple seconds looking at the kitchen clock with my coffee cup in my right hand. It would take me an hour of driving east to get to the farm and who knows how much longer to grab the raccoon. Then I would need to drive three hours in the opposite direction to get to his mandatory meeting.

Could I get to the farm, remove the animal and still make it to headquarters on time? Should I even attempt it?

I knew the smart thing to do was just relax. Turn on the TV, finish my coffee, maybe make and enjoy a big breakfast and then sit down and polish my boots some more. I could waste another half hour looking for lint on my uniform or checking my shave and sideburns. The morning would float by like I was on vacation.

After a couple hours of doing just about nothing, I could head off to the meeting. I'd get there in plenty of time and I'd look good too – just like he wanted.

But I had spent the evening before with a can of polish and a brush in my hands. I'd already shaved. I was as ready as I wanted to be.

And what if that raccoon was diseased? What if the family had kids who were handling it? What if it had scratched their dogs or cats or bitten some of their farm animals?

Everyone thinks rabies is the big threat. But raccoons also carry a deadly kind of roundworm, along with leptospirosis and salmonella. Just the dust from raccoon feces – years old – is dangerous. The disease doesn't make the raccoons sick. But humans? Inhale it and you can die. There's no vaccine and there is nothing doctors can do to save you if you become ill.

This animal was being kept in a cage, the caller said. That meant urine and feces were concentrated there. Was someone going into the cage and cleaning it up without wearing a mask and gloves?

Play it safe and just wait? Or do what people were paying me to do and go?

I put my coffee cup in the sink, buttoned my shirt, grabbed my gear and the paperwork I needed for the meeting and ran out the door to my cruiser.

I made good time getting to their mountain home, even though I bumped so hard over some potholes I was concerned I'd tear the exhaust off my cruiser.

I arrived to find the usual mix of barking dogs, skinny barn cats, a couple of saddle horses with burdock knotted manes and tails, a cow and calf,

a dozen wandering chickens of various colors
and sizes and several geese. All of them – except
the horses, cows and cats – made a lot of noise
announcing my arrival.

I had hoped to look around a bit and maybe spot
the raccoon. But with the racket, I knew anyone
inside had been tipped off to my arrival.

I decided to just walk up to the front door about
50 feet away.

I reached for my hat and stepped out of the
cruiser and that's when it hit me – the pungent
smell of pig. It was like an invisible cloud of hog
on the hoof had enveloped me.

My eyes watered and my stomach flipped and I
was glad I hadn't eaten a big breakfast.

I glanced to my left and saw a pen 70 feet away,
a little hidden by trees. I could see pink noses
pushing against the wire. If they were calling to
me too, I couldn't hear them above the din of the
circling geese and barking dogs.

I put my hat on hoping the wide brim would
act as an umbrella to keep the stink off me and
walked quickly towards the house.

I didn't get very far before a couple in their thirties

stepped out onto the porch to greet me.

I didn't have time to beat around the bush. I had to remove the raccoon and head to my meeting in Waterbury.

"I'm Game Warden John Kapusta," I told them. "I was told you are keeping a raccoon as a pet. You can't do that. It's illegal. I'm here to remove it."

The woman pursed her lips, crossed her arms, nodded and looked down at the porch floor. The man said nothing and just watched her.

"If I have to get a search warrant and come back here, you will end up paying a fine, maybe going to court," I told them both.

"Let's just get this over with right now. Where's the raccoon?" I said, trying to speed her along.

The husband's eyebrows had shot up at the words "fine" and "court" and "search warrant." He leaned into her and gave her a little poke in the ribs with his elbow.

She nodded as if she understood him.

Her shoulders rose and she wiped an eye. "The kids will miss Rocky," she sighed, looking at me. "But yes, it's the right thing to do."

"Where?" I demanded again.

"Over there," she said pointing off to the right.

I turned and followed her arm, hoping maybe I'd spy a nice clean cage with a gravel walk leading to it. And maybe the cage would be under some trees to give the 'coon and me some shade. The sun was rising by the minute and the barometer with it.

Standing in the driveway with the sun in my face, I felt beads of sweat on my forehead. I wanted to stay cool, make the boss happy with my spotless appearance at the upcoming meeting. But it was sticky hot and only a little after 9 a.m.

I was counting on this raccoon removal to be quick and clean.

No such luck.

"All I see is your hogs," I said.

"Yes," she said. "He's in the pig pen, in the back. It's a good, strong cage. And Rocky loves to eat, so we put him in there."

A raccoon in a pigsty?

I briefly considered asking the husband for help, to keep the pigs back. But I realized he might just get in the way or worse, get hurt. I was used to doing things myself.

"All right then," I said and nodded. "I'll take care of it."

I turned and strode briskly to the back of my cruiser. I unlocked the trunk, reached for my catchpole and headed to the pen to take a look.

The pole was a six feet long piece of copper pipe with some airline cable running through it to the handle. It wasn't a fancy one like they have today, but it worked the same.

You could make the loop whatever size you needed to get it over the animal's neck. Once you snagged it, you pulled the cable taut with your other hand at the pole's base. When you had the collar around their neck, you could pretty much move the critter wherever you wanted it to go, especially the little ones.

This tool was a huge improvement over lying on your belly under a crawl space trying to grab a fox, raccoon, bat or bird with nothing more than speedy reflexes and thick leather gloves. Gloves and short arms was a good way to get yourself a trip to the doctor, after being scratched or bit bad.

But even with the pole, you had to get the

timing right.

An animal might think it was just a tree limb coming at them the first time you extended the pole and noose. But once they figured out you were trying to slip a noose around their neck – watch out.

You might fool them once, but if you had to keep at it, get ready for a battle.

As I approached the pig pen, I spied a sea of snouts – some big, some small, some pink, some spattered with mud – all of them jostling up and down, pushing at the sides of the wire pen braced with pallets.

And just when I thought it couldn't really get worse, it did.

The pigs were standing in earth stomped into brownie batter, at least eight inches deep. There were shimmering pockets of pale yellow liquid decorating their pockmarked paddock. The pools caught the sunlight filtering through wilted trees. The puddles shimmered, shook and splattered as the porkers ran at me.

I had a good idea what those yellow stains were, along with a lot of dark piles dropped willy nilly throughout the pen. I made a mental note to steer clear of the pools and piles – to treat them all like landmines.

And in front of me, the porkers pushed against the gate like a pack of noisy puppies. A human coming near meant food. Each wanted to be first in line.

There were at least 20 pigs. The majority were youngsters, maybe 25 to 60 pounds. But there were four giants waddling towards me, nodding their heads up and down and grunting. These hogs were 250 to 350 pounds each and needed to be taken seriously.

The little ones raced around like pink comets, leaping and crowding each other and screaming bloody murder when a bigger pig pushed them back.

Of course, the more they stomped up the muck, the worse the stench got. My eyes watered as I looked beyond the porkers and tried to spot a raccoon.

Atop the slop were three boards laid end to end, each eight feet long and six inches wide. They led to a shed gate. It made sense that the sows with the newest piglets were housed in there before being allowed to race about with their larger cousins.

And at the end of that shed I saw the corner of a crude cage. It appeared to be made out of 2x4s and chicken wire and it sported a wood and wine roof.

"That's to keep the raccoon from climbing out," I told myself. "He's gotta be in the back there."

The walkway lumber had aged gray, was twisted and cupped from all the moisture coming up from the ground and the rains and snow above. The middle board seemed to be reaching for the sky. It was bowed on each end. The boards lay on top of concrete blocks. The mud had almost swallowed them up.

The planks looked to me like they would rock considerably. But it was the only way through the churned earth paddock.

It was clear the pigs liked walking the planks too. The boards were dotted with mud, urine and feces – not necessarily in that order.

I thought back to the days when I would walk the fat rusty cables of the Danby marble quarries to give myself a thrill. I'd stand 200 feet above the rock pit – arms extended to help me balance – no net. Some would say "no sense."

How hard could walking a few six inch wide

boards a few inches above this pig mess be?

If I got a little mud or worse on my boots, I could find a rag and wipe them down before the meeting. Having put in the time to make them shine, I was serious about being presentable later today.

The real trouble was the pushy pigs were watching my every move. They knew the routine.

I knew the worst thing you can do is stand still when animals start mobbing you. Do that and it's easy to get knocked down and trampled. Act like you're in charge, keep your feet moving and you've a much better chance of staying on your feet.

So, I unsnapped the clasp, told the mob of porkers to "Shoo!" and planted my right boot on the first plank.

My catchpole went inside and I swung it back and forth like a pendulum to prompt the pigs to move back from the gate and me.

"Get back! Go on! Shoo," I said over and over.

The pigs parted like I was Moses at the Red Sea – a frothy wave of pink and white and gray, grunting and squealing in irritation as they leaped out of the way. But unlike the Biblical tale, these waves turned on their heels and raced right back at me, again and again.

I ran. The boards bounced, but I stayed upright
with the help of the pole, which parted the pigs
and kept them from tripping me up.

When I got to the three foot high shed gate, I put
my arm behind me and kept swinging the pole to
keep the porkers' snouts off my pant legs. I was
trying as hard as I could to remain spotless.

I stepped over the shed's metal gate and pulled
the catchpole after me.

As expected, there were a couple of sows inside,
each in their own stall. They jumped to their feet
when they heard me coming and pressed their
noses against the heavy planks.

I saw a rough wooden door 16 feet away and
walked over to it, put my ear to the door
and listened for a few seconds. I heard faint
scratching inside.

I smiled slightly. I almost had him.

I let out a few inches of wire to form a noose on
the catchpole. I didn't want it very big. Maybe
three or four inches in diameter, but plenty big
enough to slip over the head of an unsuspecting
12 week old raccoon. If he tried to slip by me, I

wanted to be ready to snag him.

Tick tock. Tick tock. Tick tock.

In the back of my mind was my boss's dirty
look and the lecture I got the last time I was late.
"I'm tired of excuses. One more time and..." kept
replaying in my head.

I pulled the door open just wide enough for me to
slide inside. I kept the catchpole low.

If this baby 'coon made a dive to wriggle out, he'd
put the noose around his own neck, like a rabbit
running into a snare.

But there was no dive. No sound of movement
either. I stepped slowly inside, pushed the door
shut behind me and looked around.

When I saw him, I stopped dead in my tracks
– in awe.

Sitting on the stout limb of a dead tree inside
the wire pen was the biggest raccoon I had ever
seen. It had to have been 40 pounds. It was so
big its belly was hanging over its hind feet and
that belly was bald.

He was like a raccoon version of Buddha, with a
mask instead of a smile.

Trapped in the cage, unable to move freely and fed like a pig – ears of corn, stale bread, donuts and milk – he'd swelled into a giant.

I looked down at my catchpole. I felt like the fellow in "Jaws" searching for the mythic shark. When he finally spied it, he muttered, "We're gonna need a bigger boat."

Looking at that monster, I felt the same. This was no baby raccoon. He looked more like a silverback gorilla. He had to have been kept as a pet for years.

What were the odds he'd go quietly?

I replayed the conversation I had with the caller as I slowly released more and more and more noose wire.

The informant never said how big or how old the raccoon was. And I hadn't asked. Same with the property owners. I'd just assumed it was a young one.

I made a note to myself, "Sometimes it pays to ask for a few details."

The animal eyed me carefully. He swayed left and right on his perch, his belly oozing along above hind feet I couldn't see. He was trying to determine if I was a friend or a foe.

I didn't speak. If he heard my voice, it might spook him more. Better to be silent, I figured.

I took a few steps closer and reached out with the pole. He was so accustomed to humans, he didn't think twice about me or it coming at him.

He reached up with his two front paws like he wanted to grab the stick. Maybe the family had fed him marshmallows or hot dogs or ears of corn this way?

I got the noose about six inches above his head and while his arms reached out looking for food, I let the wire loop fall over his head in one swift move, right onto his furry collar.

He looked down at the wire like it was a shiny necklace to admire and began to reach for it. Before he could touch it, my left hand yanked the wire and the noose went tight around his neck.

He blew up like a hand grenade – 40 pounds of rippling silver, black and gray furry fury.

His eyes popped wide open. He sat up straight and screeched in anger, yanking me forward. He grabbed for the tree like a napping cat refusing to leave the sofa. He wanted to stay put.

Beneath that fur coat and fat was muscle and lots of it.

I knew I was in for a real battle. There are stories of raccoons defeating hounds four times their size. This huge rascal was going to show me how it was done.

I turned sideways to have more power. I yanked – once, twice, three times – to pull him free of his tree.

It worked. He dropped to the bottom of the pen and landed on his feet like a giant cat. His hair went straight up, making him appear twice as big. He arched his back, showed his teeth and snarled like he wanted me to believe he was a grizzly bear.

He was getting ready to charge, to fight me. I didn't have time to ease his fears, to tell him about how much he would enjoy a life away from his cramped 'coon condo and maybe make friends with others of his kind.

I opened the rough door, backpedaled out of his cage and through the sow shed as fast as I could, skidding him along the earthen floor.

He hissed and screamed in rage. The pigs jumped to their feet when they heard the scuffle

and began grunting, their snouts sniffing the air.
They peeked between the boards and watched
me struggle.

The raccoon sat on his backside and dug his
claws in. He scratched the floor like a wildcat.
Looking behind him, it looked like a harrow had
run through the sty.

When I reached the low metal gate, the bustling
pork pack was there – snuffling, grunting,
leaping, squealing and banging. They'd heard
the commotion and were agitated even more
than before.

It struck me I was in a spot of trouble. The pole
I'd used to push them out of my way was now
busy, wrapped around the neck of the giant
snarling raccoon.

I stopped for a few seconds, trying to figure out
what to do. And my dead stop gave old Rocky a
welcome break.

He rolled onto his back, grabbed at the noose with
his front paws and kicked like a windmill with his
back legs trying to push it up, off his neck.

The raccoon screaming, the fact I'd come in and
not given them the grub they expected or both,
had stirred the pigs up even more than when I'd

entered their pen.

There was a sea of angry pink in front of me,
squealing and jumping up and down on the
planks in and out of brownie mix slop – so fast
they were a blur.

I realized there was no way I could skid that giant
raccoon along those planks behind me. He and I
would get tangled up in pigs and slop and lumber.
He might bite or claw one of the porkers and that
would cause even more problems.

I'd have to carry him.

I stepped up to the metal gate, turned to face
the planks and the pigs, bent my knees, pulled
the catchpole a couple feet closer, laid it across
my right shoulder like a baseball bat, then stood
up straight.

The raccoon was livid. He twisted and shuddered
and swung his body left and right, kicked up
and fell back down. I felt like I was hauling
a writhing python.

His long tail slapped my back and the claws on
his hind paws scratched the back of my shirt.
I didn't like how close he was, or that I couldn't
see him, but I sure didn't want to look back either.
I just knew I had to make a run for it.

Only there was nothing to push the pigs away from me now. All I had was my voice and my boots. The pole was behind me with the 'coon reluctantly riding it.

"Get back! Get outta here! Go on! SHOOO!" I shouted at the porcine posse.

I couldn't even wave my right arm. I had to hold onto the pole with both hands to keep the noose tight and the pole atop my shoulder.

But I needed the pigs to get out of the way as I ran along the planks. I waited a split second for an opening, kicked at the gate to create a rattle and scare them off the gangplank, then made my move.

I stepped over the gate, put a heel down and took off running, growling, "Get outta here!" hoping to scatter the pigs.

And it worked. The little ones scrambled. The big ones bolted. They all got out of my way, but not without consequences. When they leapt on and off the planks they turned the boards into a trampoline.

It felt like an earthquake beneath my boots.

I ran. I bounced and my reluctant passenger bounced along behind me. And everything was going pretty good for the first 10 feet or so.

Maybe it was me shouting at them. Or maybe it was seeing their neighbor, the raccoon, floating above them like some giant, angry Macy's Day balloon. Maybe, it was the sound of him gasping for breath and hissing in rage.

Instead of running and staying gone, the curious pigs circled back. Some stopped dead in their tracks and stared at the raccoon hovering above them, their eyes wide and mouths open. Others rushed in to take a closer look.

The confusion caused a pile up – a terrible tangle of pork tails, hooves, bellies, snouts and ear piercing pig screeches – at my feet.

For a count of two, it looked like someone should call a wrecker. Little piggy bodies and giant hogs were all laid out.

I stopped. The only place I had to put my feet was on top of a piglet. The plank rocked like I was a tightrope walker attempting to traverse the Grand Canyon and a wind gust rocked me.

The raccoon felt the change and twisted in rage. His swung his lower body, reaching for my hat, my hair, my collar with his back feet. He was just inches away from sinking his rear claws into my neck.

I yelled again at the pigs, "Get out of my way!!" like I was a thundering storm cloud. In a count of three, they were all back on their feet and the wooden path opened before me. I waited a split second longer for the board to stop rocking.

I looked back and pushed the pole away from me a few inches. I didn't want that reaching raccoon to get hold of my ear. I turned back and stepped forward, without looking first.

Problem was, the piggy pile up had prompted a few porkers to leave some frightful piles behind.

My boot stepped into what I like to remember as mud.

But looking back on this incident, I know it was darker, wetter and a whole lot slipperier.

Rocky twisted like a big mouth bass slamming a frog lure, just as my boot slid.

And maybe they'd planned it, but one of the 300 pound hogs came up behind me and pounced on the board to look more closely at the struggling raccoon at exactly the same time.

The chain of events was too much for me.

My heel slid off. Rocky yanked his body harder to the right. My foot went up and over my head like I had lost my rope while riding the biggest, baddest bucking bull in the string.

The raccoon and I both went up into the air. He noticed the change in the pressure around his neck and leaped, pulling my arm out and straightening my back.

I landed like a cow flop in the pig slop.

I was ear deep in the pig pounded pudding, still refusing to let go of the pole. I didn't want the raccoon to get away after I'd come this far.

He might have had his Buddha belly buried in pea soup, but he was not a quitter. He dug his claws into the filth, tugging hard and wriggling – trying to get free of me.

It was like I was night fishing from shore and had slid down the bank into the soup, trying not to lose a massive fish.

But ponds don't have pigs.

I heard snorts and oinks circling my head, saw snouts and muddy hooves and pieces of blue sky and clouds. Down or dead, the pigs were determined to go through my pockets for food.

I waved my left arm about and shouted out a few choice, "Pigs! GO AWAY" phrases and they spun on their hind hooves and took off. And when they did, their hooves kicked more filth into my face.

I sat up and threw myself forward onto my knees and pulled my right arm in closer, so I had more control over the raccoon. He was squirming and hissing and glaring at me.

I pulled my knees up, bent at the waist, threw my chest forward and got onto my feet. I ignored the gangplank, gritted my teeth, lifted the pole with the mud soaked raccoon back up onto my shoulder and stomped the final 12 feet through the muck to the gate.

The pigs came back, running after me. They were all around my feet and poking my pant legs with their snouts. I didn't care anymore.

I told them to get away from the gate, yanked it open, slid my body out while hoisting Rocky too, latched it and didn't look back.

I walked to my cruiser like Frankenstein. My boots were coated with pig pen goo and weighed three times what they usually did. My pants and shirt were stuck tight to my skin. I was soaking wet and covered with mud and much worse from my pant cuffs to the top of my head.

I lowered the still squirming raccoon and the pole into the trunk and slammed it shut.

I walked to the driver's door, opened it and slid inside. I didn't want to drive feeling like I had a wet diaper, but what choice did I have?

And when I did park myself behind the steering wheel, all the sopping wet pig stuff was driven up into my trousers and shorts. I leaned back against the cushion and despite the thermometer hovering around 87 degrees, when the slop pressed through my shirt and the entire length of my spine, I shivered – not from cold, but stomach churning disgust.

If it sounds bad, it's because it was. I was plastered with pig, from boots to hat.

I pulled my door shut, turned the ignition key, spun the cruiser around and raced out of there.

I didn't want to think about how filthy I was. How it was all seeping into my pores and into the car seat and worse, into my skin. I had a three hour drive ahead of me to make the meeting with my boss.

But I still had one more thing to do.

I pulled over about 15 miles out, peeled myself
off the seat, opened the trunk and let my
passenger out.

He was calmer thanks to the heat and the dark.
And I took advantage of it.

I lifted the pole, carried him to the road edge with
trees and green grass beckoning him, set his hind
feet on the ground and slid the noose wide open.

He wriggled and his head slid free. He shook
himself from nose to tail, then waddled off
towards the trees. I knew there was a stream
100 yards inside those woods.

I was envious the Rocky would be taking a shower
before me. But I had to get going.

I tossed my pole back in the trunk, shut the lid,
shook my shirt and slapped my trousers to try
and knock off more of the mud. Then I jumped
back behind the wheel and took off as fast as I
dared drive.

I pulled into the office parking lot and smiled.
My shirt and trousers could pass for dry, thanks
to the wind racing through the car. The green of
my uniform was more a clay color, but at least I
didn't look like I'd gone through a car wash and
forgot to roll up the windows.

I turned off the cruiser, looked at my watch and was delighted to see I had arrived with eight minutes to spare.

I looked at my face in the rear view mirror and saw I needed a little work. I spit on a paper napkin I had stashed in the ashtray and wiped a few flecks of mud off my face and flicked gray globs off my shirt collar.

There wasn't time for more sprucing up. I grabbed my papers, jumped out of the cruiser and ran towards headquarters, through the door, up the stairs, and hustled down the hall to the conference room. I heard clumps of dried mud fall from my boots as I trotted down the waxed floor of the hallway. I made a mental note to find the janitor and apologize later.

I waltzed into the meeting with a minute to spare and smiled to myself. I saw my boss glance up at me briefly as I entered, but I didn't make eye contact and I didn't say a word to anyone.

I took a seat – right next to a stack of paperwork 13 inches high at the head of the table. I knew that would be where my boss planned to sit and lecture us.

The other fellows looked at me sideways. I wasn't certain if it was because my uniform wasn't quite

up to snuff or it was the odor following me
– or both.

Maybe they were just surprised I had actually
made it to the meeting on time.

I took my seat and dropped my papers in front
of me and put my hands under the table. I knew
my fingernails were caked with mud and my
shirt cuffs were filthy too. I wanted to keep
them hidden.

My boss walked by me, took his place at the
head of the table. I watched his lips moving as he
silently counted heads, then looked up at a big
wall clock.

When the second hand touched the hour, he
called the meeting to order and began to dig into
his agenda items, a big smile on his face. He was
never more in his glory than reviewing piles of
paperwork with us.

Within five minutes, the fellow in the seat beside
me was squirming. I knew what it was. The pig
perfume I was wearing had begun sifting through
the room.

My fellow warden used the ruse of dropping his
pencil under the table and diving for it. I didn't
move. But he sure did.

You would have thought the pencil had legs and had run off.

When he was done chasing it around the floor and came up for air, I noticed he had scootched his chair out a good 14 inches away from my elbow. He was practically sitting in the next fellow's lap.

Ten minutes later, the warden across the table from me made a face like someone had tucked a dead skunk in his boot. He ducked his chin, cleared his throat and raised his eyebrows at me. He reached into a pants pocket and pulled out a handkerchief and briefly held it to his nose.

I didn't buy into any of the silent accusations. I kept my head down and stared at the papers and just let the boss drone on. When it was time to turn the page, I did. I behaved like the perfect schoolboy.

He stood up about 15 minutes on and stepped back from his chair to address us, papers in hand. That was unusual for him. But maybe he had a leg cramp or just wanted some exercise?

A half hour in, with the windowless room warmed further by the hot July sun beating through the drawn shades, I wondered how long this meeting would go.

The boss had scheduled the meeting for the entire
afternoon – nearly four hours.

Could he do it?

An hour into the meeting, I noticed my fellow
wardens had pushed themselves an arm's length
or more away from the table. Their faces looked
like someone had stashed an infant who needed
a fresh diaper beneath our table.

The boss was acting odd too.

Every once in awhile he would lose his place, his
head would snap back and he'd look startled
– like he had just gotten a whiff of something foul
and it rocked him.

He glanced sideways at me a couple times, knitted
his brows and scowled. I pretended not to see the
dirty looks.

As miserable as I was in my pig slicked duds and
sticky underwear, I sat up straight, didn't squirm,
didn't smile, didn't say a word.

I'd done what my boss had ordered me to.
I'd shown up on time for the meeting. No excuses.

An hour and twenty minutes into the meeting,
he couldn't take it anymore. He stopped talking,

then suggested we all take a little break. He said we would reconvene in 15 minutes.

He left the room and the other fellows scooted out of there behind him – fast.

I stayed right where I was.

I didn't want to be dropping more pig powered mud around the building or give my boss a chance to really look me over. I just wanted to get through this. The clock couldn't spin fast enough.

Fourteen minutes later, everyone straggled back in looking like they'd been assigned septic tank cleaning duty.

There was none of the usual "ha ha ha" from the fellows with one another. They clearly didn't want to come back into the stifling conference room.

Once everyone was assembled, my supervisor walked to the head of the table, held up a single piece of paper, cleared his throat and surprised us.

"I've been called away and must attend to this important matter immediately," he announced. "I am terribly sorry. But I am needed. This meeting is adjourned."

And with that, he ran from the room like he had

an urgent need to visit the men's room.

My fellow wardens jumped to their feet and hustled out the door after him like they were sixth graders during a mandatory fire drill. They didn't speak.

I stayed in my chair another minute, until I was certain everyone was gone. Then I looked up at the clock and began to smile.

My porky pig bath had cut his duller than dirt sermon short by nearly three hours.

I almost felt like doing it again.

Almost.

*"I plunged into the icy water
and tried not to gasp."*

Willoughby Baptism

Contributed by John Kapusta

I came to think the world of Warden Don Collins. He was a fellow who could do just about anything he set his mind to. And whatever he chose to do, he would do it to the highest degree.

He wanted to be a trap shooter, so he spent a couple years practicing and eventually won the state championship.

Then he decided he wanted to race snowmobiles. He bought a machine, modified it, practiced and practiced his riding so he could shave seconds off his time. And he eventually won the state championship for that sport too.

He was a guy who had to stay busy. He loved to carve wood, especially ducks. And, of course, that took a lot of time to perfect. Like you see women who keep their hands busy knitting at Town Meeting, Don might just be in the woods, see some random little stick beneath a tree and pick it up. Then he would pull a little pocketknife out of his pocket, and within a couple of minutes, still walking, he would turn that little branch into something beautiful, into a work of art.

One time a bunch of us were sitting around a campfire shooting the breeze and one of the fellows had a new pencil in his pocket. As a kind of joke, he handed it to Collins and said, "Let's see what you can do with this."

Don didn't say anything. But he found his penknife, moved a little closer to catch the firelight, bent lower and went to work.

With a few strokes, he carved an entire duck in the little bitty pink eraser. When Don was done, he handed it back to the fellow who had given it to him. He shook his head and passed it around. The duck looked so real, you woulda sworn it would get bored sitting there, want to rejoin the flock and just fly off the pencil.

But all this came later. It would be years before I ever called Warden Collins by his first name and got to know him well.

I first met him when I was a trainee, assigned to work under him. He was my boss and becoming a full time warden depended on my doing a good job for him. If he didn't like my work, didn't think I had what it took to be a good warden, I could be sent home.

I was determined to make it.

Don Collins worked the Barton area, not far
from the Canadian border. I was from southern
Vermont, so the area was new to me.

It was early Spring, with snow still refusing to
melt under many cedars and pines. The ice
had retreated from the shoreline, but there were
still large, thin sheets floating on the main body
of Lake Willoughby. Ice fishing had been over for
a month.

Yet it was far too early to think about boating.
You'd be inviting disaster with logs and ice
lurking just beneath the surface. They could
easily bend a prop or worse, rip a boat hull like a
can opener.

Even though it was too warm to ice fish and too
dangerous to go boating, Willoughby still offered
some good fishing for the hardy souls willing to
brave the last gasps of winter. Spring meant
rainbow trout were on the move, headed to their
spawning grounds.

It was legal to fish for them on the main lake,
but not in the streams that fed into the lake.
The brooks were off limits, to give the fish a

little privacy.

After all, those big rainbows were busy setting up housekeeping to raise the next generation.

So as a warden in training, my new boss explained it was important for us to check this area once, or even two and three times a day, to protect that fishery. And regardless of where anglers were fishing, a warden always has the right to demand they show proof of a valid fishing license and their catch. It being a new year, some fellows might have forgotten to renew.

Doing this work allowed my new boss to see how I was in both handling myself in the woods, along steep shorelines, as well as dealing with the public.

So, one or more times a day, Warden Collins would drive and I would ride beside him in his cruiser, to check on anglers trying the waters of Willoughby.

I'd been on the job with him only a week or two. He was tight lipped about how I was doing.

But as best I could tell I was doing okay. There hadn't been any problems and all the fishermen we'd encountered had been friendly or at least cooperative.

Many of them seemed to know my boss and would say things like, "Breaking in a new fellow there, Warden? Don't be too hard on the youngster!" and chuckle. It was nice to see he had a good rapport with the people in his district. Though, I admit it was a little tough for me to be noticed right away as the new recruit.

But the friendly attitude of folks fishing Willoughby changed unexpectedly one sunny, cold day.

We had again driven to a pull off where we could hike to a fishing spot where the main lake met one of the mountain streams used by the spawning trout. I hadn't been to this one before. It was new to me. But there was a good footpath to follow.

Don accompanied me down the path.

We had to duck through trees and watch our footing for a quarter mile or so. There was some snow, and mud covered slopes. And you didn't really see much of the lake until the trees gave way to brush, maybe 50 feet from the shore.

I really didn't expect to see much fishing once we got to wherever he was taking me. The wind was bitterly cold and the while the sun was getting high in the sky, it was just not strong enough to generate much warmth. Winter was still very much in charge. I didn't think anyone would be fishing in this weather.

We came around a bend and stepped out on top of a clearing. I immediately spotted three guys wearing insulated chest waders, casting over their shoulders, trying to catch some big rainbows.

They were standing probably 70 feet out into the lake and maybe 50 feet from where the stream entered Willoughby. It struck me it was a little odd to be fishing that deep into the lake. It had to be cold even with insulated waders. And if they fell in, they could really be in trouble. But they weren't breaking any laws from what I could see.

I figured my boss would want to watch them for a bit, then we'd turn around and head back. Or maybe my boss would want to wait until they came into shore, then we'd check their licenses and their catch.

I stood there a few seconds in silence, until my boss said to me, "Why don't you ask those men to see their licenses?" It was like telling a bird dog to find the birds.

I studied them. I saw these guys were getting their money's worth from their chest waders.

They were practically armpit in the water – so deep it made it hard for them to cast.

Their line would catch the water and the droplets would spill off and catch the light like little diamonds falling.

The three men appeared to be between 40 to 50 years old. I didn't see anything suspicious about the way they were acting. And they weren't in the feeder brook which would upset the spawning trout and was against the law.

But if the boss thought I should make certain they each had a valid Vermont fishing license, it wasn't for me to question him. Maybe he recognized one or more of them? Maybe he had cited them earlier?

I knew enough not to question the boss, even if it meant these fellows were going to have to wade all the way back into shore for me to do what I was told.

And that is never easy in Spring's fast moving New England waters. It is nothing like sloshing your way along the smooth bottom of the shallow end of a swimming pool. The floor of most Vermont lakes are strewn with deep mud, sharp rocks – and in this postcard famous lake – van sized boulders.

Add to that minefield, there's thick, calf wrapping, ankle grabbing, greasy weeds. And to top it all off, there's the occasional rotting tree stump, just waiting to trip you up and pull you down into the drink so you can study the entire murky mess first hand.

And if all this detritus doesn't tank a wading angler, the rushing lake currents swirling around their legs surely could. To fish Spring waters, you have to plot your next move carefully, and you had better know how to swim. It's difficult and why most people don't chance it.

Fall in while wearing chest waders?

Waders fill quickly with water. It can be impossible get the snaps loose and climb out. Every year experienced fly fishermen drown before they can wriggle free. Knowing and seeing these men fishing icy Willoughby on this brisk day, I said to myself, "These guys must really like lake trout."

And to be that far out into the lake? "They must have a good idea where the trout are to take such a chance," I said to myself. "It would be easy to fall in and tough to get out. There has to be some swift currents out there."

I walked down the ridge a few feet to get in front

of the shrubs so the men could see me clearly, stood up straight and announced, "Game Warden. I'd like to check your licenses. Please, come into shore," with a smile in my voice.

I waited for their response. The three of them just kept fishing, acting like they hadn't heard me.

Well, I thought I had put enough air behind my vocal chords, but there was a wind blowing. After waiting 20 seconds with no reaction from the trio, I took a deeper breath and tried it again, louder.

"Game warden! Please, come into shore. I want to check your fishing licenses," I shouted out over the water again and confidently waited for them to turn around and start wading towards me.

But they didn't. It was like they hadn't heard or seen me.

I felt my cheeks turning red with embarrassment.

I knew my boss was just 20 feet behind me, watching my every move and listening to every word. I could feel his eyes burning a hole in the back of my head.

"What is up with these guys?" I silently asked myself. "They had to have heard me! Why don't they just come in?"

I felt my temperature rising, despite the sky beginning to spit wet snow in my face.

I didn't mutter under my breath or stamp my foot or give any outward indication I was perturbed.

I worked hard to be professional. I was not going to let those guys get to me or let my boss see that they were.

I decided to try it again, even louder.

I cupped my hands around my mouth like a megaphone and took a huge, deep breath like I was shouting across the lake to somebody over in Barton.

"GAME WARDEN! I WANT TO CHECK YOUR LICENSES. COME IN! NOW!" I bellered.

Two of the three men turned their heads just a quarter turn. They gave me a "What's his problem?" look, scowled, shrugged their shoulders, looked again at each other, turned their backs to me and cast anew.

I saw the third guy turn his head and mutter something to the other two and all three laughed so hard I could see their shoulders shaking.

Well now, I'm mad.

I tried to think of reasons why they would not cooperate with me. Was it my uniform? I was pretty certain it was perfect. Here I was trying to do a good job and these fellows could ruin it for me, get me thrown out of the program.

Why were they doing this?

Maybe they were onto some good fishing and didn't want to spook the trout by stirring up the bottom and walking out? Maybe the bottom was so slippery it took them a good amount of time to get out that deep and they just didn't want to come in yet? Maybe they didn't have valid licenses?

I didn't know. They weren't talking to me. But they sure weren't respecting my uniform or the law.

I trotted gingerly down the bank and stood so close to the water it was lapping the toes of my boots. "COME INTO SHORE NOW!" I commanded them.

The guy in the middle of the pack turned and scowled at me, like I was a nuisance –a barking dog on the shore – interrupting their fun.

He looked right at me, scowled, shook his head "NO," and turned back to his fishing. Then his buddy looked over his shoulder and yelled out, "Kiss my behind, Warden!"

The third guy joined in, "Go home, Fish Cop! Leave us alone!"

The insults began flying at me fast and furious once they started: "What's your problem?" "For cryin' out loud! We just got here!" "Get lost!"

I didn't turn around to ask my boss what to do or even look at him. I knew I was supposed to figure out how to handle this situation myself.

I thought briefly about just waiting for them to come in. Even wearing insulated waders, how long could they stay out there?

The water was 46 degrees, maybe less. The air was just 52 degrees and here they were standing chest deep in a half frozen ice cube tray. They might be dry, but the cold should force them out soon. They'd be popsicles in an hour or so.

I could just wait for them to come in. But that wouldn't say much about me, other than I didn't want to get my feet wet.

Their insults were getting louder. They were pointing at me, still slinging barbs and laughing harder.

I'd had enough.

I tore off my jacket, unbuckled my gun belt and laid them on the ground. I removed my portable radio, emptied my pockets, took a deep breath and charged into the water like I was a lone Arctic hunter, miles from home, who had just spotted his kayak drifting away with the current.

I saw my dream job drifting away if I didn't get those guys to do what I asked.

WHOOSH! I plunged into the icy water and tried not to gasp.

I was sorta okay for the first several steps but when the ice water hit certain tender areas, it was quite a task to force myself to keep slogging. My brain screamed, "GET OUT OF THE WATER!"

The three of them heard the sound of a grizzly bear charging them from behind. They wheeled around and just stared at me.

"Ggggame warden! Sssshow me your ffissssshing li-iiii-cen-sessss! NnnOW!" I shouted when I got within 25 feet of them.

My teeth were chattering so bad I was beginning to have trouble talking. My legs felt like someone was pricking them with 15,000 pointy toothpicks.

My toes were tingling something awful – the ones
with any feeling left in them.

I was trying to remain polite, but the faster they
showed me their licenses, the better.

All three stopped insulting me and pulled out
their licenses – the lake water was splashing
all around me – some of it landed in my mouth.
I looked at all three pieces of paper quickly, trying
not to let them see me shiver. They were fine.

"I should write each of you up for failing to exhibit
your license upon demand of a game warden!"
I growled at them through chattering teeth.

The three of them stood there like statues. They
didn't say a peep. After all their insults? That
was odd. Why weren't they still being wise guys?

I saw their eyes drift upwards, over my head, back
to the shore where I had left my boss standing.

Now, that I was standing still in the water – just
the current and wind cutting around me – I heard
something back on shore. It was muted, but
getting louder.

It was my boss. He was laughing like I had
seldom heard anyone laugh – I believe the term is
"hooting." If an owl had a sense of humor,

I guess someone a long time ago thought an owl would sound like Warden Collins when he saw something amusing.

And it was contagious. Because now the three men were breaking into spits and sputters and manly giggles. I turned my head back towards shore and saw my boss give them – maybe me too? – a thumbs up.

And once the fishermen saw him signal, their mood instantly went from "Get lost!" to "Geez, Pal, you're gonna freeze to death! We gotta get you outta here!"

They went from mean uncles to doting aunts in an instant, it seemed to me. They said things, "Buddy, you gotta get outta here now. It's soooo coooooold in this lake! We didn't know if we could last out here waiting for you to show up! Come on, we'll help you. Let's go!"

And all four of us waded in as fast as we could into shore, making certain to give one another an elbow to lean on now and again, so no one fell in.

Collins stood their chuckling, hands on his hips and shaking his head as I worked my way out of the water with the three anglers.

I was dripping Willoughby ice water, seaweed

and silt. I'm certain I looked like one of those embarrassing pictures of Fluffy the cat, snapped right after she climbed out of the fishbowl.

Once on shore, the fellows locked their reels, started to pull their rods apart and looked up at my boss. One fellow said, "Man, that water is sooooo cold!!!!" while another asked, "Well, Don. How'd we do?"

I'd been played like a fish, a young one. The trio were great friends of my boss.

I'd been set up to see how I'd react when faced with a challenge.

The fishermen and my boss were all talking and laughing. But I couldn't. My teeth were chattering too hard. I just hoped if this was part of my on the job training, that I'd passed the test. But I knew I shouldn't ask. For all I knew, the test wasn't even over yet.

I looked around for my gun belt, radio and jacket and was about to walk over and get them. But my feet felt like chunks of firewood and I wasn't certain they'd cooperate.

My boss saw what I was looking at, ran over and scooped up my gear for me and said. "I got it. I'll carry it for you. Let's get back up the trail and into the cruiser so you can warm up."

"You go ahead, Don," one of the anglers told my boss. "We'll follow you to camp as soon as we get out of our waders."

"Camp?" I didn't say anything, but I definitely liked the sound of that. A place where I could get out of these soaking wet clothes sounded great.

My boss and I hustled back to the cruiser. He popped the trunk and grabbed a piece of canvas for me to sit on. And once I was seated he draped a heavy wool blanket over me, then jumped behind the wheel and cranked the heat on high.

A short ride away, he pulled into a narrow driveway, up to the door of a tidy cabin. When he swung the camp door open, I was hit with a welcome blast of heat. There was a glowing wood fire burning in the hearth. For the first time that day, I broke into a big grin. I was going to be warm soon.

I took off my boots, got out of my wet clothes and put the wool blanket back over me. I stood dancing from one foot to the other, close to the stove.

And when the three fishermen arrived, they handed me a stack of clothes – BVDs, trousers and a couple warm shirts and two pairs of thick socks for me to put on. They had them all ready for me in a back bedroom.

The five of us had a big lunch with bowls of chili, warm bread dripping with butter and cups of steaming hot coffee.

Of course, most of the talk was them regaling me with how I looked before and after I jumped into Willoughby like a polar bear after a seal.

But it was all in good fun.

By the time the meal was over, I felt like I was among friends.

It was like I'd been baptized somehow.

And being the new guy in the area, doing my best to earn a coveted spot as a game warden, that meant a lot to me.

Warden Collins didn't say a lot. He smiled and laughed, ate some chili but mostly listened. He let his friends do most of the talking that day.

He didn't tell me whether I passed his test or failed it.

And I didn't ask him.

But when I fell into bed that night, I felt pretty good about how I'd done that day.

And you know what I said earlier about Warden Don Collins? About him being top flight at anything he put his mind to?

About him having the ability to focus his energy, put his all into something and be one of the best?

Well, as I learned that day many years ago – long before I knew him well enough to call him my friend – Warden Don Collins also excelled at field testing the new guys.

105

"I heard Walt say, 'Get down out of there,'
and wondered what in the world he was
talking about. I found my deputy standing
beside an old apple tree and grinning."

106

Concord Chase

CONTRIBUTED BY KEN DENTON

I t was crazy warm for October, just a couple weeks before the opening day of bow hunting season. I stepped outside with a cup of coffee around 7 a.m. and felt it immediately.

The air was charged – like a thunderstorm was building – headed right for me.

In northern New England, a balmy day this late in the year gets people feeling frisky. And a some don't stop just because the sun sets early.

I picked up the phone and called Deputy Warden Walt Ackerman. He was scheduled to accompany me this night.

"Can you believe this weather?" I asked him.

"No. We sure don't get many days like this, this late in the year," he agreed.

"I think we could be busy tonight," I said.

"I had the same feeling," Walt chuckled. "Got a plan?"

I told Walt I thought we should head to Peacham, to a road where we'd caught poachers before. And I thought this would a good night for Snickers, my female black Labrador, to come along.

I took pride in the fact no guy had ever escaped from me on foot. I always caught up with them.

But I had to admit, I was getting a bit older. I knew if I brought Snickers, she'd make certain my record stayed intact. No poacher was going to outrun her. She'd lead me to them.

That night, Walt and I were in Peacham with Snickers. We were set up in the corner of a dark field, watching for any sign of poaching in progress, when a call came over the radio that a shot had been heard over on the Concord Road, about six miles away.

You have to be both fast and lucky when you get a "shots fired" call. You don't want to go storming over, lights flashing, siren blaring.

You need to sneak up on poachers and outsmart them.

I got us over there in about six minutes, slowed

my truck to a crawl, kept the lights on and rolled the windows down. Walt and I looked carefully at the road shoulders for any sign a vehicle had turned around quickly or entered a field.

Braking hard, turning the steering wheel sharply and roaring off – produces distinct tire marks. When wardens sees fresh signs of a U turn on a dirt road, they ask themselves, "What made the driver turn around in such a hurry?"

Sure, maybe somebody forgot their wallet and needed to go back home, but that's pretty rare.

Even then, most drivers would wait until they got to the next driveway to turn around. That would be safer.

So, why would you take time to reverse direction late at night in the middle of a back road?

There were some very small fields off the Concord Road. They were too small to even be called fields, really. They were more like grassy areas shaped like bowling alleys – if bowling alleys were edged with trees instead of gutters. What they were good for, was late night deer feed.

And for poachers, that meant opportunity.

Walt and I looked and listened. The night air was

still eerily warm.

We didn't talk. We didn't need to. Stealth was the name of the game. We'd done this hundreds of times over the years.

Walt spotted fresh tire tracks leading between some trees, into a narrow green. "There!" he whispered.

No pointing, no arms outside the vehicle. No heads turning or nodding. No jumping up and down in the seat making the truck wiggle like a kid who spotted a lost hubcap. And I certainly didn't touch the brakes. Nope. My truck just kept the same steady roll.

From outside the vehicle, there was no indication Walt had seen anything. If someone was tucked away in the woods, worried, watching us drift by, they would believe we'd missed the clue. They'd think they were in the clear.

And that's exactly what we wanted.

But I trusted Walt's eyes and instincts and was already onto our next move.

I knew the hidey holes along this road where a truck could slip in and not be seen. There was a summer residence set back from the road, with a heavily treed driveway leading into it, a hundred yards north.

We'd use that property as our base of operations.

I slid the truck up that driveway quietly, parked it close to the house where no one would see it from the road, and shut off the engine.

Walt and I got out quietly, making certain to keep the noise to a minimum, and prepared to walk back to where he had seen the fresh track, about 70 yards away.

I snapped the lead line on Snickers' collar. Walt and I grabbed our flashlights and the three of us hurriedly strode back down the road towards the field where we had spotted signs of recent entry.

It was dead quiet.

The night didn't feel anything like October in northern Vermont, when we'd usually see our breath and hear beech tree leaves rattling. With Halloween a few weeks away, the weather and woods felt strange, unnatural.

I used my flashlight but kept the beam trained down, never up. We didn't talk. We didn't want anyone hearing us. We wanted to surprise them and pounce.

We got back to the field entrance, bent low and studied the tracks more closely, with hands cupped around the light's lens.

Walt was dead on.

The prints were fresh and there was only one tread pattern. That told us either a vehicle had exited the grassy area a short time ago or a vehicle and the occupants were still inside.

So, which was it?

Walt and I gingerly stepped inside. Snickers was right beside me. The three of us slid as quietly as we could into the meadow, taking three steps and then stopping to listen for any sound that might indicate someone was nearby. Now, we used the moonlight only to search. No artificial light.

Nothing. No vehicle. No sounds of anyone about.

But within 100 feet, Snickers began tugging on the lead, telling me she was onto something.

I let her pull me like a divining rod towards the forested edge.

When she stopped, she looked at me and flagged her tail slightly, from side to side. I knew what she was saying. She smelled fresh blood. She wanted to lead me to the deer.

I whispered to Walt. "You stay here and watch for them. I'm going with Snickers to find it."

Walt nodded and turned to hide and watch from inside the trees.

Snickers tugged me east along a wildlife trail leading to the Connecticut River. But after 100 feet, then 150, still no deer.

The clock was ticking. I knew whoever shot the deer would be back here very soon, looking to grab their prize and go.

Walt and I needed to be ready for them.

I pulled Snickers off the scent, turned and the two of us hustled back up the trail to find Walt.

Walt heard me coming and stepped out of the shadows. We agreed he would remain hidden while I ran back up to the truck with Snickers. She had done her job, proving a deer had been shot and finding the blood trail.

Now, it was time to catch the poachers. I didn't want her in the way.

Walt sidled up to a wide tree trunk 10 feet off

the meadow to wait and watch. Snickers and
I slinked along the meadow's edge, then got out
onto the road and trotted towards the truck, as
quietly as we could.

But my gut feeling about running out of time
was right.

I heard the unmistakable low rumble of a truck
engine coming for us, maybe a quarter of a mile
away. In a night game of cat and mouse, that
is close.

I hoped Walt was already set up in the woods.
Because if the poachers decided to shine a light
into that field and he was still moving, they would
spot him and bolt.

Just as bad, I was a long ways from my truck and
with my dog to boot. I had to hide Snickers and
me fast.

I jumped into the puckerbrush in three big
steps and we landed just 12 feet from the road's
shoulder.

I signaled Snickers to lie down beside me, tucked
myself up like a wooly worm, and waited.

The engine sound got louder. I saw the headlights
coming for us. I held tight to Snickers' collar,

pressed her body against my leg, and put my other hand on top of her head to keep her down. I didn't want any eyes reflecting in those headlight beams.

As the vehicle approached, I worked to memorize the details and count the people inside.

It was an older Chevy Blazer. I was too low to count heads. But just by how slow the rig was traveling, I was certain it was the poacher's car.

Now, the big question was, would the driver turn into the field or roll on by? I waited.

When the driver turned the front wheels to enter the field where Walt was waiting for them, I smiled. It was like watching dominoes fall. I knew the vehicle and plate number now.

We were one step closer to nabbing them.

But I still needed Snickers back in the truck. So, once the taillights slid into the meadow, she and I took off again up the road.

We'd made it about 150 feet up the road, when I heard the same car engine again. It was behind me and coming on fast.

My mind was racing. "What in the world? Why is the driver coming out of the field? He couldn't have located and loaded the deer that fast. What is this guy doing? Did they spot Walt? Are they outta here for good?"

My poor dog must have thought I was nuts.

I jumped over the ditch again, took two big steps and made myself into the smallest ball I could, head down. Snickers was tight beside me, her chin on the ground.

We were maybe 15 feet off the traveled lane.

If the Blazer driver caught my shadow in the periphery of his headlights, he'd floor the accelerator and Walt and I would be done. We could never make it to the truck in time to race after him.

I held my breath and waited.

The driver didn't stop and he didn't speed up. I breathed a sigh of relief when his rear bumper was 20 feet past me. I was convinced he didn't see me.

Did he drop someone off in the field to search for the deer?

If he did, is that fellow headed towards Walt? Should I keep going, trying to get Snickers back in the truck? Or should I turn around and go back?

If there were runners in the field looking for the deer and they discovered Walt, they'd take off. We'd likely never be able to catch them.

I decided to stay still and listen for a minute.

I stretched my legs a bit, let Snickers raise her head. I scratched her behind the ears. But I didn't move my feet. I was listening for footsteps coming down the road or crashing through the woods.

Instead of footsteps, I heard the Blazer coming back down the road again.

I was dumbfounded. Poachers don't generally behave like captains guiding a whale watch tour – circling back over and over.

Whoever was behind the wheel was supremely confident no warden or neighbor was curious enough to follow up on the gunshot a half hour earlier.

I'd never encountered a driver like this. He drove up and down the road at a crawl a few more times, making it impossible for me to risk racing up the road to settle my dog back into my truck.

I was losing too much time. I decided to just keep

Snickers with me and go find Walt. Together, he and I would come up with a plan.

The next time the driver floated past me, I counted to five, got to my feet, stayed low and scuttled across the road with Snickers.

Now, I was close to where we'd found their tire tracks and not far from Walt.

I found a place to stand, so I could look into the Blazer's cab at a better angle the next time the driver drifted past me. I needed to know how many guys were inside that rig. And if I could spot weapons – maybe they would have a rifle barrel sticking out the window – all the better.

Sure enough, within five minutes, the Blazer was headed towards me again. I saw the shadow of the driver all right, but the rear windows were tinted and most of the way up.

It was impossible to see the passengers. But this time the Blazer's brake lights glowed. I heard a door open and a few seconds later, it quietly clicked shut.

The taillights went dark, one at a time. That told me someone had just walked past them.

I listened harder. A second door opened and

closed. Now, I knew at least two people had exited the car.

A few seconds later, the brake lights went off and the Blazer rolled off down the road again.

Every warden knows this trick. The driver drops off one or two guys and drives away with the intent of circling back. He will pick up his buddies and their bloody prize, in an hour or two.

Walt and I were more than happy to let the guys go get that deer.

We wanted them to find the carcass and drag it up to the road and have it ready to load into the Blazer.

It would mean a lot less work for us, and a much better case against them.

Because, when wardens leap up out of the dark to nab guys covered in sweat, deer hair and blood standing next to a waiting vehicle, it's just about impossible for them to come up with a story claiming they were not poaching.

So, I was thrilled to see we finally had fellows going after the downed deer. The problem was, they were headed right for me and Snickers. And just 40 feet farther down the deer trail was Walt.

There was no way to quietly move out of their way. They were headed right for us.

We were about to be had. Snickers could chase one, but both? They'd split up. And I didn't want to lose either of them.

If one escaped and circled back to signal the Blazer driver and warn him, our entire case would be dead.

My mind was racing trying to come up with a way to intercept these guys without blowing the case. My portable radio sounded. "They're headed right for me," Walt whispered. "What do you want to do?"

Good question.

I heard their boots parting the tall grass. There was a tiny spark headed for us – a light they were shining, to follow the blood trail. But I still couldn't see the poachers. It was too dark, with too many trees and too many shadows.

I had no idea if these guys were carrying rifles and handguns.

To jump out and shout, "Wardens! Hands up!" sounds good on paper, but it's a very bad idea. It can startle some fellows so badly they grab their guns and start shooting.

So, I whispered to Walt, "We're gonna charge them. No noise. Get ready."

I waited until the sound of their feet was 20 feet away from me.

"On the count of three," I whispered into my radio for Walt's ears only. "One... two... THREE!"

I don't know if Snickers could count or she was just tired of being reined in. But she reared up and tore off after those guys like a race horse who hated starting gates.

She lunged forward and my arm followed. She bounded over the brush again and again, or tried to – but her lead line snagged on the saplings and thick vegetation.

I was losing them. Within eight seconds, I was chasing ghosts. They were gone.

I pulled up on Snickers' lead, stopped and listened, trying to get a clue as to where they had gone. The sound of feet pounding the ground and pant legs sifting through tall grass had evaporated.

I guessed I'd done too good a job of scaring them.

They were history.

Now, I had no car, no poachers and no deer I could tie them to, after nearly two hours of leaping in and out of ditches playing hide and seek.

Making arrests in this case was looking mighty unlikely.

I had also lost Walt. Where in the world was he?

I listened for him. Nothing. And that's when hope crept back into my head and I began to smile. I knew my deputy. Walt was a determined man and he had long legs. Maybe, just maybe, he could catch up to these guys and salvage this case.

I didn't bug him by calling him on the radio. I just waited and listened with Snickers sitting patiently beside me.

A minute, maybe two, of silence. Then I heard a cry off in the distance, 200 feet away, outside the narrow field.

"Here! They're over here!" Walt called. He was taking a chance shouting to me, but I hadn't heard the Blazer's engine since the poachers ran away.

I headed Snickers quickly toward the sound of

Walt's voice, through burdocks and goldenrod and into and over ditches and up a little incline and finally, there he was.

I heard Walt say, "Get down out of there," and wondered what in the world he was talking about.

I found my deputy standing beside an old apple tree and grinning. Even in the dark, I could see his pearly whites.

In the tree were two guys. One of them had made it almost to the tippy top, his back pinned to the flaky gray bark. The other was situated a bit lower with his knees drawn tight to his chest.

They both look terrified.

As I walked closer, their eyes got bigger. They rocked back and forth and the tree shook with them.

"What are you guys doing up there?" I asked them.

"The dogs!" the fellow highest up said – pointing at Snickers standing beside me. He was rail thin and pretzeled up – his legs tucked up under his chin, his elbows at his shoelaces.

"Dogs!" he said again. "All we heard was panting and dog tags jingling and lots of feet. We thought a pack of rabid dogs was chasing us!"

I looked down at Snickers. I'd become so used to her metal tags clinking one into the other, the noise didn't even register in my head.

And panting? Well, it was a warm night and she was a tracking dog that has been reined in way too many times tonight.

But a rabid beast? This nice chocolate lab?

It was hard not to laugh.

"Well, climb on down here, one at a time and raise your hands over your head once your feet hit the ground," I told them.

When we had the pair in front of us, I looked closer. They were young, between 17 and 22, probably. I didn't say anything, but I figured the driver would be about the same age.

"Who's driving the Blazer?" I asked them. Each man pursed his lips and lowered his head, and refused to look at Walt or me.

Walt and I knew we didn't have time for an interrogation. We had to get these guys out of there if we were to have any chance of catching their chauffeur.

Walt put each man in handcuffs, using the pair he had and borrowing the set I carried on my belt too.

It's hard to run with your hands behind your back. Psychologically, it works wonders to calm a fellow down. We couldn't risk having either of these two fellows attempting to make another escape.

"Let's get 'em up to the truck," I said to Walt, who told the men to start moving and fast.

"And don't either of you guys make a sound. No talking!" Walt cautioned them. "Just go."

We hiked them through the tall brush parallel with the road, through the saplings and tall weeds.

We couldn't risk walking in the road because we didn't know when their buddy was coming back for them. If we were spotted, it was game over. And headlights can shine a looooong ways.

But before we could make it to our truck, sure enough, the Blazer came lugging down the road again, at a crawl.

And now there were five of us needing to hide from him – Walt, Snickers, me and the two fellows in handcuffs.

"What else can go wrong?" I was asking myself.

"Get down! Get DOWN!" I hissed to the handcuffed men. Walt made his crazy, angry face for emphasis. He got up under their noses and growled like a deranged pirate, "Not a peep!" and raised his arm implying he would clobber them if they so much as burped.

Snickers ears perked up as she heard the distress in our voices. Her head went low and her eyes focused on the pair like they were two inch thick steaks sizzling on a summer grill.

I didn't discourage her. I was hoping they still thought my dog might have rabies or even just friends with rabies.

We needed these guys to hold still and be totally silent.

The Blazer drifted past us slowly and this time, I noticed the tailgate was down.

It was clear the driver had stopped somewhere, jumped out and readied his rig for his buddies to leap out of the bushes and slide the deer carcass in the back, close it up fast and disappear.

We waited.

Would he stop? Would he see us in the shadows cast by his headlights into the weeds?

The Blazer rolled past with no change in speed, brake lights glowing red.

There with no indication the driver had heard or seen the crowd hunkered down in the weeds and shrubbery 20 feet away from him.

We'd survived yet one more case killer. I could breathe freely again.

The question now was, how soon would he be back?

And just how was I going to get ahold of him?

"With every convoluted run, his goal was
to beat me back to the Blazer, jam those
keys into the ignition and drive away."

GIMMEE THE KEYS

CONTRIBUTED BY KEN DENTON

I was grateful this driver was persistent. He reminded me of a fellow fishing from his boat. The guy's line gets snagged but he refuses to give up on retrieving his expensive lure. A fellow like that will spend a half hour maneuvering his boat up and down the water, tugging every which way to free it.

But every angler knows there comes a point when you just have to cut bait and move on.

I knew if this driver didn't see his buddies real soon, that could happen. He had a lot more to lose than a lure.

Like wardens, poachers rely on their intuition too. If he got a feeling something was wrong, he'd be gone.

I wanted the captain of that big old boat of a car.

But if his buddies were any indication, he was not going to give up just because I jumped in front of his vehicle like a school crossing guard and shouted, "Halt! Game Warden!"

How was I going to get ahold of that driver?

I put Snickers in the truck and walked back to confront the fellows Walt had caught.

I looked hard at the two young men, studying them. One was about 5' 10" and wearing a black hooded sweatshirt. I'm about the same height, same build.

I had an idea.

"Give me your sweatshirt," I told the guy, whose head jerked up in surprise. "Walt, uncuff him for a second, so he can take it off."

The fellow looked at his buddy in fear as Walt released the cuffs.

"Do it!" I told him. "Take it off NOW!"

He wriggled out of it and handed it over to me. Walt put the cuffs back on him and secured both men to the truck's roof rack.

I motioned to Walt that I wanted to talk to him. We walked a few feet away, where the two fellows couldn't hear us but we could still see them.

"You stay here and keep those guys quiet, okay? I'm going after the driver. If I need you, I'll call you on the radio."

"Got it," Walt said and walked back to the clipped runners. I took off running, the hoodie in my hand.

I ran 100 feet, stopped at the road edge and pulled the sweatshirt low over my shirt. I yanked it as low as I could to cover my gun, radio and holster.

To make the jersey baggy, so it wouldn't outline my gear, I grabbed a fistful of fabric and pulled it way out. Lastly, I yanked the hood and stretched it, then pulled it up over my head.

When I let it go, the fabric fell over my brow, covering my eyes. Necessity and adrenalin had turned a Large into a 3XL.

When I was done, I could've passed for a medieval monk, at least from the waist up.

I was still wearing my uniform trousers. They were made of a slick fabric and had a distinctive, reflective stripe down the outside middle of each leg.

And below the trousers were my shiny black boots.

If he spotted either in his headlights, he'd be gone.

I had to time this "meet and greet" perfectly.
I went over what I had to do in my head. "He
can't see me below the waist. He can't spot my
flashlight or my holster on my side. I can't let him
see my eyes."

I also had to ask myself, "Does he have a loaded
revolver on his lap? Maybe a loaded rifle pointed
towards the passenger door? A hunting knife
beside him on the seat?"

I had to consider the danger, but not let it stop
me. The bottom line was I had to get hold of the
guy behind the wheel to make a case here.

I ducked into the bushes by the side of the road,
sat on my heels and waited for the Blazer to
return. I had my flashlight in my left hand, very
low and slightly behind me.

I couldn't have his vehicle reflect anything I had
on me. I had to appear to be dressed in flat
black, like his buddy.

I took a few deep breaths, tried to slow my heart
rate. I wanted my breathing to be normal, like I'd
been patiently waiting.

It didn't take long. In a few minutes, the Blazer
was headed back down the road towards me.

I waited until the headlights were so close he could not see me below the waist. Then I jumped up and signaled him, waving an arm over the windshield's passenger side. My head was bowed.

The Blazer's taillights came on. He stopped.

I moved immediately for the door. I didn't give him a second to look me over. I acted like I belonged inside that vehicle.

I popped the handle, my head still low so he could not see my eyes and jumped onto the seat.

My flashlight rose up like a sword at his cheek and I hit the on switch to blind and startle him.

"Game warden! You're under arrest!" I shouted in his ear from two feet away. I pulled the hood down with my right hand so he would understand I was not his buddy pulling some late night practical joke.

And now that I could see the fellow, I recognized him. He was a local football star. His photo had been in the Sports pages all through his high school years.

He was tall and strong and according to what I'd read in the paper – fast. Real fast.

His shoulders slumped and the look on his face went from touchdown victory pass to interception agony. His head fell to his chest. He didn't say a word, but his dejected look said, "You got me."

I was thinking this was finally turning into a good night's work. But you never want to jinx things by getting ahead of yourself. You have to take it one step at a time.

"Shut off the car," I told him. He reached for the keys and did what he was told. The engine went silent.

I kept my light on him and reached with my right hand under the sweatshirt for my handcuffs.

I didn't want this young man attempting to run away like his pals had. But there was only air where my cuffs should be. I'd forgotten Walt had borrowed mine to corral this driver's friends.

Not good. "Things just got complicated," I said to myself.

I tried not to scowl. I did not want him to see I wasn't happy, that I needed to improvise.

There was a console in the middle of the Blazer – a big hump. I couldn't be tossing a leg over that plastic barrier, crawling over it into him and trying to tie him down somehow.

Worse, I couldn't sit there confused as to what to do next to subdue him. I had to keep going, stay in charge of the situation.

So I told him, "I want you to get out of the vehicle and just stand next to the door. Slow!"

He reached down and popped open the driver's door latch. I turned right and pushed the passenger door open fully.

I was keeping my eyes on him though, not certain he'd comply.

For this to work, he had to accept that he was now under my control.

My left foot was inside on the Blazer floor. I was working to synchronize my moves with his, watching him out of the corner of my left eye.

He lowered his head and turned his left shoulder towards the night air. His left foot came off the floor mat, he turned left at the waist.

I looked right, taking my eyes off him for a split second.

He threw his upper body back into the cab, bent

low, twisted the ignition key, pulled the shift lever into Drive and floored the accelerator.

I caught it all out of the corner of my left eye as I was stepping out. I'd never seen anyone start a car so fast. He was a blur, with the reflexes of a cat.

The Blazer leapt forward like a napping deer stepped on by a hunter.

I realized immediately I was in huge trouble and grabbed on to the closest piece of car I could lay a hand on.

I was half in, half out of his Blazer. My right hand was gripping the doorjamb at the roofline. My right boot toe was plowing up the gravel road shoulder.

Gravity or centrifugal force – some force of Nature – was attempting to spill me out of his cab and into the night.

I probably looked like a hot dog water skier using just one ski. Only this wasn't water, this was terra firma terror. And the night was black.

I knew if I jumped, I was not going to land in a lake. I would come face to bark with one or more trees and very likely land beneath the Blazer's spinning wheels. I could die.

I bellered at the kid, "STOP THIS CAR! YOU ARE UNDER ARREST!"

Maybe his coach screamed at him all the time. Maybe his Dad did too. Maybe his whole family yelled. Whatever the reason, he didn't slow down or talk back.

I heard the front bumper slap brush and saplings at the road edge. The sound grew louder and the slaps faster.

THWACK!

THWACK THWACK!!

THWACK THWACK THWACK!!!

I could tell he was picking up speed by how frequently the trees slammed the opened passenger door, my only protection.

He turned the steering wheel further, the right tires riding the road's gravel edge. He was trying harder to catapult me out of his car.

I saw a shadowy blur of armed pickets coming at me. They were trees – saplings from two to four inches in diameter with loads of branches

– coming at my head.

There was a big mirror on my passenger door, the kind guys use when towing. It helped deflect some branches away from me. But not all.

How long until he slammed my door into something more substantial?

The passenger door swung in and out as I fought to get back inside the car.

I realized I was caught on something. I certainly had the upper body strength to lift myself up and throw my body back inside the Blazer. But some piece of my clothing or gear was caught.

I knew it was only a matter of time until my door bashed a tree with no give to it.

Hit a big enough tree and my elbow would fold. When that happened, the door would slam into me. It would knock my left hand loose from the doorjamb, maybe even crush my fingers.

What was stopping me from swinging inside the cab? Was my leather belt caught on something?

My revolver and holster sat on my right hip. They weren't the problem. I couldn't risk reaching behind me to figure out what was holding me back. I needed both hands to hang on.

I kept trying to rip myself free, twisting and turning as best I could.

I knew if I let go or tried to jump out, the door would knock me back and the trees would likely push me under the Blazer's wheels.

Letting go could be fatal. The only safe place for me was back inside that cab. But time was not on my side.

We didn't wear protective vests back then. If a small tree or branch came crashing through the car door window or whipped up from below the door, I could be stabbed, maybe even run through like a spear.

I was stuck. I held onto the thin, upper rail with my flashlight still jammed in my left hand and my right hand on the door's armrest.

I was holding onto each as if my life depended on it – because it did.

"STOP THIS CAR!" I yelled again at the driver.

He didn't.

I was working really hard to not fall out, to

get back inside, to come up with a plan to save my life.

And mixed in there somewhere, I suppose I was praying for a miracle.

And finally, I got one. Not an idea, but a miracle.

I think it was a pothole. Or maybe a simple bump in the road. Or maybe it was a confused frost heave sprouting early.

Any northern New Englander knows frost heaves. Long before there were astronauts going to the moon, there were people riding over back roads in April going a little too fast.

Back roads can turn into Nature's original thrill ride, a kind of backwoods' roller coaster. You hit a frost heave and your vehicle goes down and then everything inside it pops up, including passengers, cups of coffee and a year or two of dust.

This was the same feeling – a dip and then a gravity defying body toss – for just a split second.

The Blazer chassis plunged into some hole and then bounced up like old cars with bad springs do.

And whatever invisible hand had a death grip on me let go.

I didn't hear a rip, but I immediately felt the difference. I bounced up about three inches and for a split second – I was an astronaut.

My tether was gone. I could move freely again.

I dove onto the car seat, slamming the door behind me.

I leaned into the driver, holding my mag light chock full of heavy D cell batteries right under his right eye and waggled it like a club.

I screamed in his ear – a drill sergeant with a bad toothache – "STOP THIS RIG RIGHT NOW!"

He didn't turn his head or move his eyes to look at me. He didn't wince. He didn't speak. He kept his hands at 10 and 2 on the steering wheel.

But his right foot moved.

The Blazer's wheels locked up and the old car skidded to a neck snapping stop. He leaned back and sat upright like a statue, hands still on the steering wheel. Eyes forward.

I stayed in his face. I wasn't done.

"TURN IT OFF!!!!" I shouted at him – the flashlight waving back and forth in front of his nose.

He reached for the key and turned off the ignition.

I took a deep breath and said calmly, slowly, "Good. Now, let's try this again. Step out of the car."

He started to slide out and I turned my head to the right, like I was stepping out my side, trusting him, but I had a funny feeling about the guy. He still hadn't said a word.

I was thinking, "Is he going to go for the key again?"

If he dove back inside to try it, I wanted to be ready for his rattlesnake strike at the ignition.

Sure enough, his right hand flew for the key. He wasn't done trying to escape.

I slapped the back of his right hand with my flashlight and growled, "Don't you dare touch those keys!"

Looking back, I shoulda hit his hand a lot harder.

He yanked the keys out of the ignition and clutched them tight to his chest, just below his chin.

You'd have thought they were life saving pills for

his dear mother. He was not going to let them go.

It was clear, this guy would not give up. I had to get him separated from his getaway car.

While he was still smarting from the flashlight whack to the back of his right hand, I dove out the passenger door without saying a word.

I raced around the front bumper, yanked his door wide open and growled again, "You are under arrest!"

I got hold of his left arm, pulled it up fast behind his back and said, "Get out! Walk!"

I saw his eyes run up and down me as I demanded he get out from behind the wheel. He was sizing me up, as athletes do. His forearm was like a coiled steel spring, just aching to pop free. Impressive.

When he stepped out, it became even more apparent this young man had a big physical advantage over me.

He was probably 6' 4", in the best shape of his life. His arm told me he was likely in a gym, lifting weights every day.

I was in great shape too – but 20 some odd years

older and I stand just 5' 9".

I saw what I was up against. "If this arrest gets physical, I could be in real trouble," I realized. "He's already tried to kill me. If he goes for my gun..." I stopped there.

I reached under the sweatshirt for my radio, to call Walt. I wanted him here pronto to help me get this man under control.

But where my radio should be, I felt a smashed plastic case and crushed wires spilling out. Buttons dropped onto the road like busted teeth at my feet. It was like a tank had run over it.

I was shocked. Those radios were built solid. It took a lot of force to smash it to smithereens. Then it hit me – my chest was just behind it.

"Maybe I'm hurt and I just don't feel it yet?" I asked myself.

I didn't have the luxury of calling a "Time Out" to check myself for injuries. I had to get this young man under control fast. Only, I knew I was in a really tough spot.

I had no handcuffs and no radio to call for back up. And before me was a tall, strong young man silently taunting me – refusing to give me his car keys.

When we got to the rear bumper, I turned him around to face me and looked him straight in the eyes.

"Now. Give me those keys," I said to him.

He looked down at his sneakers, then put his chin up in the air. Defiant. And still not a word out of him.

He shook his head back and forth several times fast as if to say, "No."

It was like he was four years old, refusing to take a teaspoon of bad tasting cough medicine from me.

Did he expect me to jump up and try to take the keys from him?

That was not gonna happen.

I gave him three seconds to think about it. Then I gave him a choice.

There was pepper spray on my belt. I didn't want to use it, but I would if I had to.

"You give me the keys or I am going to spray you,"

I told him.

Finally, that got his attention. His head snapped back. His eyes went wide. He raised both hands to his face, covering his eyes, the keys sticking out between the fingers of his right hand.

His reaction told me he'd been pepper sprayed before. The keys were even farther away from me.

I sighed and reached for the spray can on my belt.

He saw my hand move. He twisted away, spun on his heels and took off running up the road like a gazelle.

"Great. Just great," I muttered.

I'd given this young man every chance to cooperate with me. My reward was him trying to kill me and now he was running away.

Where in the world was Walt?

I was a good runner, but I had just got all jammed up hanging out a car door and I'd been up and down this road, jumping in and out of ditches and racing around after his buddies before that.

Now, I have to chase and tackle a football hero in the dark?

"It don't seem right," as they say. But hey, that's the job.

I was not about to let this football star turned poacher get away if I could help it.

I took a deep breath, bent my knees, dug my right toe into the dirt and took off after him, kicking myself that Snickers was back at the truck with Walt.

I decided to try some old school warden communication to contact Walt.

"He's running! The driver's running!" I yelled as loud as I could up the road.

My hope was Walt would hear me and hurry down to help. The other two fellows were chained to the truck. They weren't going anywhere.

Walt was the guy with the long legs. I could use his help. Maybe Snickers too.

The driver crossed the road into the woods, ran back across the field, then back around again. He was like a rabbit trying to get away from a hound, make it to the hole and dive inside.

With every convoluted run, his goal was to beat me back to the Blazer, jam those keys into the ignition and drive away.

And I couldn't just wait for him at his vehicle. He could hunker down in the woods for hours or just run off and disappear.

I had no choice but to stay with him, keep running.

Lose track of him and this case was over.

Thing was, he was long and lanky and made running look effortless, while I felt like the 40 year old coach in a footrace with his high school star.

But determination counts for a lot. I kept after him. Around and around we went, up the road, across ditches, into the trees, back down the road.

And when I could get air into my lungs, I was shouting, "Walt! Get down here!!!"

I couldn't chance not keeping the young man in my view. If he hid, this case would be over. I had to get him in custody.

I called over and over for Walt. He didn't come and he didn't reply.

Finally, I managed to close the gap on the runner.

I got within five feet of him in the road.

"I think I can tackle him," I told myself. "I can dive and knock his legs out from under him. And when he falls, I can grab his feet and hold on tight.

Ha! He won't be going anywhere!"

I knew it was a little optimistic, but it was my best hope of stopping him. There was no sign of Walt and my legs and lungs were burning. I knew I couldn't keep up the chase much longer.

If the young man wore me out and beat me to the Blazer, he'd be gone.

So, I clenched my teeth and dove.

My arms reached way out in front of me. I was trying to get my hands on those long legs. I'd have settled to just snag a sneaker – anything to trip him up and send him sprawling to the ground.

But I was dealing with a star. He'd learned to squirm on the gridiron, had hundreds of guys try to knock him down over the years.

He turned his head slightly over his left shoulder when he heard me close in on his heels. He kicked out and pulled away, just as I dove.

He had an extra gear and I didn't. Worse, he

made it look effortless.

My hands slid down his jeans as if I was frisking him at warp speed – only I was horizontal instead of vertical.

My fingernails scraped lint from his jeans. I was like a curious kitten diving for a bird chirping outside grandma's window. Her claws rip the lace curtains and she drops to the floor.

Only a cat will land on her feet. Humans often aren't that lucky.

I slammed the road flat as a flounder, skidded six feet on my chin and drove a fistful of road dust and gravel into my mouth and up my nose.

The wind was knocked out of me. I gasped, rolled onto my back and gasped some more, trying to breathe, helpless as a beached bluegill. I couldn't scream for Walt until I got some air back into me. The only good part was I landed just a few feet from the Blazer.

I saw the young man's sneakers disappear again into the woods.

"He's gonna get away!!!!! Where in the world is Walt?" my brain was screaming as I gulped the warm night air.

I staggered to my feet with my sides aching and listened again for my runner.

I heard footsteps coming down the road. Was it Walt? Was help here at last?

No. It was the slap of sneakers. It was the Blazer driver circling back to his getaway car again.

He knew I fell on my face.

He had turned back around, emboldened. He wanted another chance at jumping into the Blazer, ramming that key home and roaring off down the road into the night – a free man.

I brushed my sleeve against my chin, spit out some gravel lodged between my lower lip and teeth.

My chest ached, my palms and face needed some rock picking.

I was sore from being slammed into trees while hanging out of the Blazer. I didn't like being taunted. I'd about had it.

But I wasn't about to quit.

I got to my feet and started running again. It wasn't pretty. It was more like staggering at the onset, but I kept my feet moving ahead.

And that's when I saw something strange, about a mile ahead of me, up in the sky. It was a faint glow where there never was one before – like there were streetlights over the hill.

Only I knew that wasn't right. There was no town over that way. I kept after the driver, following his crashing through the woods.

I smiled even though it hurt to do it. But I didn't stop running. I kept the young man in my sights.

I still had no idea where Walt was, why he hadn't come when I had yelled to him over and over again.

But it was clear Walt had called for back up right after I left him with the young men handcuffed to our truck. And that was a smart move, because we didn't have room in our vehicle to take these guys in. And if I was lucky, there was about to be a third man who needed a ride.

I sensed maybe the driver was slowing down. Even he had to be getting sick of this game of running in circles, right?

Ten seconds later, he slammed the brakes on his sneakers and dropped into the puckerbrush at the edge of the road.

He folded his 6' 4" frame up into a baby ball

– knees to his chest, ankles and elbows crossed tight. His hands covered his mouth and nose, the keys still clenched between his fingers. They looked glued to his forehead.

I slowed, walked over to him and shone my light down. He was curled up like a January wooly bear. Finally he spoke.

He shouted, "I give up! I give up! I give up," over and over and rocked back and forth, turning his head away from me.

He was expecting me to pepper spray him. And I admit there was a part of me that wanted to let him have it.

But I didn't.

I believed him. I believed he was done causing me problems. I gave him a few seconds to roll back and forth in the road like a three year old enjoying a good tantrum.

When I'd had enough entertainment, I said, "You're under arrest. Give me those keys. Then stand up and hold still."

He peeked up at me, trying to see if I had pepper spray in my other hand. When he was satisfied I didn't, he unfurled his arms and dropped his car keys into my waiting hand.

We walked him up the road towards Walt.
My runaway was clearly done.

The state police arrived just as I was about
to turn into the driveway where I had parked
my truck. That was the blue glow I'd seen in
the distance.

They saw my flashlight shining and the trooper
who was driving rolled down his window. I asked
to borrow a pair of handcuffs.

The young man put his hands behind his back
and I clicked them on his wrists.

Finally, I was certain the driver wouldn't take
off again.

The state police – there were two of them there to
help us – followed me in their cruiser as I escorted
the driver the final few feet, to meet up with his
buddies and Walt.

I handed him to Walt, then I headed back down to
the Blazer to look inside it for a rifle.

I found some illegal drugs under the driver's seat
and a pipe. Maybe that's why the driver had been
so intent on getting away.

But I didn't find any firearms. Of course, all that driving around after the deer had been shot gave the trio plenty of time to stash the weapon at the home of a friend or family member.

I looked briefly down at the road, to try and find what had prevented me from pulling myself into the Blazer.

I found more pieces of my radio on the road. Had that been the problem? Did it get caught?

I walked back up the road. The state police had called a wrecker to haul the Blazer. The three suspects were placed in the cruiser's backseat to head to St. Johnsbury.

Things were definitely looking up.

When the state police drove away, I was finally able to speak freely to Walt.

I asked him why he hadn't come down to help me chase the driver.

"You told me to stay put with those guys," he replied. "I heard you yelling, but I couldn't make out what you were saying."

And, of course, Walt was right.

"How come you didn't just call me on your radio?" he asked me.

I lifted up the sweatshirt and showed him what was left of it. His eyes got big. He whistled and shook his head.

Walt knew it just about took a tank driving over our radios to bust them. They took a lot of abuse.

"Are you okay?" he asked me.

I shrugged. "I'm not feeling anything bad yet," I answered.

Coyotes began calling near the Connecticut River, where Snickers had tracked the deer a few hours earlier.

"They smell the blood. They're going after that deer," Walt said knowingly.

"Let's go get it and I'll fill you in as we go," I told him. It was good timing.

"Yeah, we'd better go find it fast before we have to shoot our way outta here," Walt joked.

I got Snickers out of the truck and the three of us followed the blood trail until we found the carcass. They'd shot a doe.

Walt and I hauled the carcass back and loaded it into the truck bed. If we found the rifle, we might be able to match the bullet.

Then we drove to the St. Johnsbury barracks to interrogate the three men.

They refused to tell us where they had stashed the rifle, who owned it and who had fired it. But it didn't make any difference.

We had plenty of evidence.

They were each charged with illegally taking a deer. And it got worse for the driver. When we ran his name, it was clear he was having a tough time since he graduated from high school.

There was a long list of charges pending against him for other offenses and he was already on probation. He was not supposed to be getting into any kind of trouble.

I felt bad for him really. He was a good athlete. He had potential.

In addition to the deer charge, the prosecutor added reckless endangerment and attempted escape to the former football star's charges.

The State's Attorney considered adding attempted

vehicular homicide, when he heard how the young man had tried to chase me out of his vehicle like I had been a hornet buzzing him.

But, because I was fortunate, the prosecution decided the charge would never stick. All I ended up with was a wrenched back, my radio smashed, and my right boot sole shaved a tad shorter than my left.

I was sore for a few weeks, but nothing worse.

The young man probably didn't think so at the time, but he was lucky too.

He went to jail, was ordered to do some community service and his probation period was extended another few years.

But if he had killed me, he might still be behind bars.

In the weeks that followed, I spent a lot of time going over this case in my head.

I never – ever – wanted to be hanging out of a vehicle, fighting for my life like that again.

I decided it all boiled down to handcuffs.

That's where this arrest went wrong. I'd given my

pair to Walt to use. That left me with none.

So, for the rest of my career, I made a point of carrying not one, but two pairs of handcuffs on me. And I stored extras in my truck.

Because, it's not enough just to be able to sniff the breeze, feel that tingle and know there's a storm headed right for you.

In this job, you better be ready to handle it.

"It was clear they had called in help,
pulled out all the stops, were trying
everything to get the fish to bite."

How's the Fishing?

Contributed by Denny Gaiotti

One of my duties as a warden was to help stock rivers and streams with fish raised in state hatcheries.

It was a coordinated effort with a lot of input from biologists and anglers. Mother Nature had a say as well. Rivers too high or too low meant you might have to make some adjustments with the delivery date.

But once the day was set, I'd arrive at the hatchery bright and early, climb into the cab alongside a driver with our orders for the day, and we'd be off.

Getting the fish into their new home quickly was imperative. Fish are sensitive. Just moving them from one location to another can cause some to wilt like a plucked dandelion.

We knew if we weren't careful we could end up with thousands of fish looking at the world sideways – floating on their sides, fins barely fluttering – and no way of reviving them. So, the

plan was start early and keep going until all the
fish were out of the holding tanks.

This day, I was riding shotgun alongside Jim, an
employee of the Salisbury Fish Hatchery. We were
stocking a few Ripton streams with brook trout.

Brookies are prized by backwater anglers.
They're a beautiful fish, hardy enough to eke
out a living in tiny, ice cold mountain streams
and they taste great. And while some fellows
are sticklers for native fish only, there just aren't
enough to go around.

The compromise was some areas were wild fish
only – no hatchery fish allowed – while other
streams were supplemented so everyone who
wanted to fish for them could have a shot at
catching a few.

Our truck was loaded with tanks of brook trout.
There were probably a few that weren't legal
size, but most were. That didn't mean these
fish were monsters grandpa would mount above
the fireplace mantle. Brookies are about at the
opposite end of the spectrum.

These fish were just six to eight inches long. But
they were a legal catch for anyone willing to fish
Vermont's cold mountain streams.

The way some people feel about fiddleheads are the way some anglers feel about brook trout. They're a treat.

And in the Spring, after a long cold winter, anglers who like to sit beside a stream and wet a line get serious. When the state hatchery trucks roll through towns, word spreads like wildlife.

It might start with someone seeing the tanker at the general store. Maybe we had to fill up at a gas station before heading out. Guys would stop what they were doing, turn to a neighbor and together they'd speculate as to where we were headed.

It was fun to roll past kids on bicycles and see their eyes light up like we were the best float in the July 4th parade. They'd slam on their brakes, jump off, wave and smile at us from the sidewalks and front lawns.

I knew those kids would search for their fishing poles and be rummaging around for hooks and sinkers. Others would race to grab a shovel and start digging for worms.

A few kids would shout out to us, "Where you goin'?" and pedal fast after us, like they would love to chase us all the way to our destination if they could.

I'd always give them a wave and a big smile.

Part of why we did this was to get kids outdoors.
All the better if their parents or a big sister or
brother took the time to go fishing with them.
Of course, stocking the rivers helped bring
recreational anglers from outside the state as well.

But now and again, we'd come across adults
who, when they spotted us drive by, got this
dreamy look on their faces, like they were
watching an armored truck pull away from the
biggest bank in town.

They'd spy our tanks, start elbowing each other
and put their foreheads together like they'd love
to get their hands on all that money – or in this
case – fish.

Today was one of those days.

As Jim and I rumbled down the road, being
careful not to make our thousands of passengers
in the tanks behind us seasick, I looked in the
rearview mirror.

I noticed a faded red sedan with a bumper that
sat a little cockeyed across the grill. I didn't think
much about it, until I realized the car stuck with
us as we climbed into the hills, away from town.
There weren't a lot of exit points on the winding

road we were navigating.

Was the driver following us or did he have a friend or relative up here somewhere?

When Jim rolled up on a stop sign, I looked harder into in the tanker's side view mirror. The driver and his passenger became clearer as their car crept closer to our rear bumper.

The fellows looked familiar.

I remembered I'd shone a flashlight in their faces a time or two along the back roads of Salisbury. They were two of a sizable clan, ranging in age from 16 to 80. The family all liked fishing and hunting, but some of them weren't good at following the law.

One or the other of this family had been cited for illegal possession of deer, exceeding their daily limit on fish and that sort of thing. State and local police knew the family too. They'd been cited for possession of stolen property and endless motor vehicle violations.

I had an idea of what they were up to. They wanted to follow us to see where we were stocking fish. They'd come back later with their relatives, maybe even divide the locations among the family. They would fish out all the brookies and ruin the fishing for everyone else.

Jim put the truck into gear and I turned my eyes back to the road in front of us, I didn't share what was going on in my head. I told myself it was just a coincidence they were behind us.

I was just being a pessimist. These fellows were probably just going to visit a sick uncle or call on a friend.

But the farther we traveled, the more my optimism got pushed to the side. They didn't turn off. They stuck to us, back 150 feet or so, but never leaving.

I wasn't pleased to see these fellows following the truck, but there was nothing I could do about it.

They had every right to drive the same road. I was just hopeful the sedan would roll on past us when Jim signaled he was stopping, so I could jump out and stock the first stream.

But that didn't happen. At our first stop, the car slowed and stopped about 100 feet behind us, pulling off into the puckerbrush, with the occupants watching my every move.

I pretended like I didn't notice and just got my pails, climbed up onto the truck, put water and fish into each one and slid down the bank on my

166

heels to get the fish into the brook.

It was quite a balancing act to stay upright while sliding down a bank through a tangle of saplings, berry bushes and brush with a sloshing open pail of water and fish in each hand.

I figured our stalkers would pull up to the spot I had just stocked once we left and start fishing if they had their poles in the car. If not, they would mark the spot, spin the sedan around, race home and come back with their tackle as fast as they could.

I just had to focus on doing my job – get the brookies into the streams as fast as I could before the sun made my job – and the survival of these fish – a lot harder.

I told myself these fellows would disappear from my rearview mirror soon.

Jim put the truck into gear and set off up the road around a bend readying for our next stop. He slowed the truck as I angled my neck, both of us looking for the safest location. On some of these narrow roads it was a challenge to get out of the way of traffic and still give me a safe place to climb up and down.

When Jim signaled and pulled over, I again

looked into the mirror. And there they were.
The red car was sitting behind us.

And at stop after stop after stop, they would see
the turn signal and they'd do the same, hanging
back close enough to watch us, but not close
enough to interfere.

They reminded me of seagulls following an
ocean trawler.

I'm not a guy to let stuff get under my skin, but
the more times I jumped out of the cab, grabbed
the pails, climbed the ladder, filled the 5 gallon
buckets with water and fish, stepped down off the
ladder, slid down stream banks with a bucket in
each hand – trying hard not to spill a brookie
– emptied the fish into the streams, then carried
the empty buckets up the bank to the truck,
battling brush and brambles up slippery slopes
– I felt my mood souring.

Their relentless presence began to irk me.

What had started out being a nice day stocking
fish so kids and families and anyone visiting
Vermont might have the thrill of a tug on their
line, their reel spinning and the sight of a
gorgeous little mountain fish, was disappearing
fast. It was turning what was usually a really
nice annual event into disappointment.

If they weren't writing down our stops, they were
surely taking as many mental notes as they could.
And based on my past experience with these
fellows, it was clear what they intended to do.

Jim and I were going through a whole lot of trouble
just to stock the refrigerators and freezers of these
fellows, their cronies and extended families.

But the truck was loaded, the sun was climbing
and we had a job to do.

This wasn't a job where Jim and I could park the
tanker, take a long lunch and then get back to it
an hour or more later. We had to keep hustling,
get all the fish into the streams. If the sun
heated the tank water even a few degrees, it
could mean trouble.

Over and over I went up and down filling buckets
with water and fish, battling through the brush
and emptying the pails.

And every time I'd come up out of the brook, I'd
pause to look both ways before stepping into the
oncoming lane and – you guessed it – there was
the red car's occupants sitting in the shade and
watching me sweat.

I marveled at how they could devote their day
to following a state truck around. Most people

would have chores to do, errands to run or something more pressing to do. But these fellows found me and the fish more interesting.

Jim and I kept at it for hours, with the fellows in the red car pretending they were invisible.

The sun rose and along with it, my blood pressure. Until finally, we got a break.

What they hadn't considered was the nature of mountain streams. Near the source, the roads running alongside are often dead ends. And so it was, our stalkers finally painted themselves into a corner by tailing us for better'n half the day.

We were way up in the hills of Ripton. Having gone as far as would could go, Jim was twisting the steering wheel and backing up into trees, then going forward six feet and repeating this over and over to get the big rig turned around.

It was a three point turn that really required four or more. And for the fish left in the tanks, it must have made them think they were on some sort of nauseous thrill ride.

While our followers' sedan was considerably shorter, the driver had to slide by us to get his car turned around. There was no other way for him to get past us.

I looked into the side mirror and saw the driver stop, waiting for Jim to get the big truck pointed back down the road. It was clear these fellows intended to stick with us – like barnacles on a ship's hull – for the entire day.

I decided it was time for a little chat.

"Jim, just pull ahead and then stop a few feet in the middle of the road, please. I'm going to have a few words with those fellows," I said.

"No problem," he said, smiling, like it would be a relief to him as well, if I could get them gone.

Jim made it look like we were headed down the road but when he'd driven about 150 feet, he braked and rolled to a stop – leaving not enough room to pass on either side of us.

Their car was just 30 feet off our truck's back bumper.

I opened my door, climbed down and walked on up to the driver's door.

"Well, Hello Gentlemen!" I said, as the driver rolled down his window and looked all innocent at me. "How are you today?"

We usually ran into one another late at night,

and they'd be winking as my flashlight beam streaming inside their car. I got the feeling they were trying to act surprised to run into me, like they just hadn't noticed me or the truck before.

"Hello, Warden!" they said in unison. They smiled like innocent schoolboys.

"It looks like you are interested in doing some fishing later today?" I asked.

They looked at one another, and began fumbling around for answers. "Us? Geez, no... uh... Well, maybe. We do like to fish but...."

They were already fishing. Fishing for the right words – for an answer they thought I'd like to hear. I gave them a couple seconds to squirm. But I needed to get the remaining fish into the water. So, I cut to the chase.

"Look, you two fellows don't have to follow our truck. How about I just swing by your place and dump a few pails in the brook in back of your house? Hunh? How does that sound?"

Their heads snapped back and their mouths fell open. They looked at me in shock.

Then they turned towards each other with expressions that said, "Did he just say what I think he said? Did you hear him say what I think he said?"

My offer was settling in. But it took a few seconds.

The silence was broken when the driver said, "You'd do that?"

Before I could answer, his passenger leaned over, wriggled his body between his cousin and the steering wheel, looked up at me and said excitedly, "Yeah! That would be great! Thanks!"

I had the distinct feeling he'd wanted to turn the car around and head for home a long time ago.

"Okay then," I replied. "You gentlemen head on home and I'll be by in awhile to take care of you."

"Uh. Okay," the driver said. "Thanks! We'll, uh, I guess we'll be seeing you later then."

"Yes. I'll be by," I said. And with that I nodded, stood up straight, strode back to the truck and climbed back into the passenger seat.

"Pull ahead a little and let them get in front of us, Jim. Then we'll head down to the next stop," I said quietly as I put on my seat belt.

"Got it," he said while looking left before pulling

out. When the red sedan scooted past us and disappeared out of sight, I felt like the sun had broken through the clouds.

Jim let his left foot off the clutch and we continued on our way. In a little more than an hour, I noticed a lot fewer fish were sliding out of the tank into my pails and I mentioned it to Jim. One more stop. Then another. I was running the pails down to the stream but there wasn't but a handful of fish coming with me. One more stop and there was nothing but water.

I pulled myself back into the truck and said to Jim, "I promised those fellows I was talking to earlier, we'd stop by and I'd unload a few pails in the stream near their place," I said. "They're just down the road here a bit. You okay with that?"

A puzzled look came over his face. "Didn't you just tell me you a minute ago, we were all out of fish?" he asked.

"Well, yes, the count might be getting a little low," I said slowly and winked.

"Ahhhh, I gotcha," Jim chuckled and nodded. "Well, sure! You just call it when you want me to pull over."

We drove on and in about two miles, I announced,

"Their house is ahead on the right, around this next bend, Jim. If you stop a couple hundred feet above the house, I'll take care of them."

Jim drove the tanker around the corner and when he saw the domicile come into view, he slowed to a crawl.

I saw two people sitting on the front steps. I couldn't make out their faces through the trees, but I figured it was the fellows in the red sedan, waiting for us to drop by.

I saw their heads turn towards the sound of the truck approaching. When the truck got about 250 feet above their house, I said, "Right here will do, Jim," and he stopped.

When I got out of the truck, I saw one fellow elbow the other, smile and nod. I didn't let on I was watching them. I just went to work.

I jumped down from the truck and went through my routine. I grabbed the pails from behind the cab, filled each one carefully, then crossed the road with one in each hand.

I stepped over a guardrail, slid down the bank, ducked through a tangle of saplings and brittle grasses to the stream. I put one bucket down on a tiny patch of almost level ground and poured the first pail slowly into the river.

When it was empty, I picked up the second pail and slowly emptied it into the stream.

I looked at the water a few seconds, then put one pail inside the other and worked my way back up the bank to the truck.

"Let's go on a ways," I said to Jim when I climbed back in.

"You got it," he said.

The truck rolled by the cousins sitting on the stoop. They were standing now and smiling. One of them gave a big wave towards the truck. The other nodded in satisfaction.

"Is that it?" Jim asked.

"Nope. I want to put in another two, below their house another 200 feet or so. I want to make certain they are all set," I told him.

"Good idea," Jim replied, working to keep a straight face. "Just let me find another place to pull off."

Jim drove beyond the house a few hundred feet, and I went through the routine again.

Only, I noticed when I walked down to the stream this time, several more people had come out of the house to watch me. I kept my head down and stuck to the job at hand. Our job done at last, I ascended the truck steps one last time. Jim headed us back to the fish hatchery.

It was early afternoon. I drove home to grab a late lunch and put my feet up before heading back out to check our work.

I knew word would have spread. People would be out fishing in droves. I wanted to make certain everything was going well with the fish and the public.

I would check some licenses, make certain cars were parked well off the road and just look things over, retracing the route Jim and I had traveled earlier in the day.

It was an hour to sunset when I pulled up to the home of the red sedan. I parked my truck and strolled out back.

I found a half dozen lawn chairs and lots of beer in ice filled, open coolers. There were four young men fishing. One was poking around in his tackle box, trying to find something the fish would bite. Another was casting upstream. Still another was sitting still as a statue, staring at his bobber like he could will a brookie to bite.

Another couple fellows were there, just drinking beer and watching.

It was clear they had called in help, pulled out all the stops, were trying everything to get the fish to bite.

Their heads swiveled when they heard me approach.

I called out to them as I walked towards the party. "Just came by to see how you were doing," I announced. "How's the fishing?"

The fellow who had been driving the car turned to look at me, then looked back at the stream, shook his head and scowled.

"Nuthin' yet," he said as I stood alongside him. He stared at his line and knitted his brows together like he was ready to dive in after the them. He had a look of determination on his face that was admirable.

"Anybody?" I asked looking at the others. "Nah," a fellow off closer to the stream said.

"Not yet," a younger fellow said and spit.

HOW'S THE FISHING?

I saw one man take a long pull on his beer. He crushed the can with his hand, dropped it on the ground, burped loudly and glared at the stream.

I stood and watched them for a few more seconds, pursed my lips and nodded.

"Well, it can take awhile," I said to the men. "You just keep at it."

I got shrugs and knowing nods from the assembly like I was their high school football coach and we were down 27-2 at the half.

I turned and walked back to my truck, jumped in and drove around the corner. A little smile crept under my moustache.

How long they kept their lines wet in that fished out section of the river behind their house, I have no idea.

But I like to think they stayed with it at least a couple days. That way, everyone else could have a chance at some really good fishing.

"Plates hit the table inside, silverware clanged and clinked. Feet stomped and ran on the floorboards. And hearing all that noise, that's where he aimed his fabled furry flag."

STINKERS

CONTRIBUTED BY DENNY GAIOTTI

The Dispatcher called me to say a woman was complaining about a skunk on her lawn.

"Did she say it was acting funny? Like it was sick?" I asked the Dispatcher.

"No," she replied. "I asked her. She said she just didn't want it around. She wanted an officer to come and 'remove it immediately'." The Dispatcher's voice rose to just shy of breaking glass on that last part.

Some people confuse game wardens with pest control. This appeared to be one of those times.

It's normal for skunks to go near homes looking for a meal. They eat mice, insects, worms, frogs, berries, grass and more. They are one of Nature's original pest control pros. They mostly work at night and for free. Most people never even know they're around.

The animals have very poor eyesight. Just hold

still, don't make any noise if one is coming at you and they will generally just waddle on and not even see you. It's noise and movement that scares them. Their only defense is their eye stinging, breath stealing spray.

I figured this skunk was searching for grubs in the lawn. Grubs kill grass, shrubs and flowers. And when they come out of the ground, as insects, they do more damage. This skunk was actually doing the woman, maybe the entire neighborhood, a favor.

Since the caller didn't say the skunk was showing any signs of being sick, or doing anything but being a skunk, I didn't return the call. There were a lot more productive things for me to do than hunt for a healthy skunk. I knew the animal would move on in search of another food source eventually.

So, I asked the Dispatcher to call the woman back and just tell her to leave the skunk alone. A skunk has a right to walk about, the same as a cottontail on a lawn or a moose wandering through the forest. They all have to get a meal somewhere. They can't go to the supermarket like humans.

And I hoped that would be the end of it.

But this lady was persistent. Over the next week,

she called almost every day saying she had seen it on her lawn early in the morning.

She told the Dispatcher the animal was an "unsightly presence" in her neighborhood. She continued to insist the state send someone to her home to remove it.

I could tell by the Dispatcher's voice, she was getting worn out dealing with this caller.

My schedule opened a bit and I decided to pay the woman a visit early the next morning. I wanted to politely explain the difference between game wardens and pest control. And I also intended to explain why she should just leave the skunk alone.

I thought maybe I could help her understand it was wildlife. Skunks, snakes, snapping turtles – some people may not think much of them – but they all have their place in Nature.

I studied the name and address I'd been provided. It rang a bell.

She and her husband had moved to the Middlebury area a few years earlier and did a lot to support the Arts, which was good for everyone.

I drove on over to her neighborhood a little after 7 a.m. the next morning to look around.

The street where she lived had one of those names that would lead you to believe the residents there were wildlife friendly: Blue Heron Drive, Fox Trot Lane and the like.

But of course, whatever wildlife had roamed there had been pushed out to build houses. And these homes were mammoth. A couple of them even sported turrets, like some sort of castle.

There was paved driveways, cement curbs, sidewalks, and every front yard had a threesome of deeply mulched weeping birches or some other dwarf ornamental type of tree. There wasn't a dandelion anywhere.

I recalled when the land supported a small dairy farm 25 years earlier. It had been in the family for generations. But when the old man died, the kids had no interest in working seven days a week. They sold the place and the houses went up not long after.

Generations of skunks, weasels, foxes and more would have roamed that land to find an easy meal while the farm was operating.

The skunks would have found beetles in the hay and grain, grubs, berries and all kinds of vegetables tossed to the edge of the gardens. They could even steal kibble left out for the barn cats

or dogs. And just as important, they would have
been able to burrow beneath the sheds and the
old dairy barn's foundation to make a safe home
to raise their young.

But no more. With the farmhouse and barns
bulldozed, they and a lot of other wildlife had
lost reliable food sources and their homes.
No skunk could burrow through the poured
concrete foundations of these homes and garages.
They'd been locked out, banished.

I didn't see any dogs or cats roaming about.
Only a few cars with blinding shines were parked
in the odd driveway. A couple of men wearing
suits and ties were seen hustling to their cars,
headed to offices somewhere. But there weren't
any kids waiting for a school bus or people out
walking their dogs.

It was like a nicely manicured ghost town.

I rolled on up to the address I'd been given and
took a closer look at the house from the street.

It was the biggest one in the development,
with pillars on either side of the front stoop.
The house had a copper roof, several stories and
a turret to boot.

I thought back to the farmhouse and people I had

known. Family members would gather there in the evening, wave to the neighbors and watch over their kids playing in the front yard. That was something these houses didn't have.

I looked at my watch. It was just 8 a.m. I pulled into the driveway, parking to one side so as not to block anyone coming out. I shut off my truck, took a deep breath and exhaled, put on a friendly smile, reached for my hat and stepped outside.

I knew this was not the kind of neighborhood where visitors were expected to come to the back door and knock. I walked to the front door, between the pillars and admired the work. It was some exotic, dark wood with leaded glass panels and hammer forged hinges. The door was about nine feet high and a foot wider than most homes.

There was a shiny brass lion head knocker in the center just for show. To the right was a doorbell that sported a button all lit up in the middle of the day. I pushed it.

Chimes sounded inside, trilling up and down the scale like a musical waterfall.

Within a couple minutes the door opened and a 40 something year old woman with perfectly coiffed hair, wearing a dress, high heels and lots of jewelry opened the door.

It was clear I had not interrupted her mopping floors or cleaning the oven.

She looked carefully at my uniform and then said, "Are you here to take care of the…" and stopped before she finished her sentence.

It was as if she couldn't even say the word "skunk."

She made a face like she had sucked on a lemon and then continued "… the wild animal?" and her chin rose.

"I'm Vermont Fish and Game Warden Gaiotti. Yes, Ma'am," I answered.

"Well, you have certainly taken your time getting here! I've been waiting for days for someone to come deal with this problem," she said in exasperation. "And now, I have friends coming to play bridge in a little more than an hour!"

"And you drove here in…?" She leaned out the front door and looked right into her driveway and spied my state truck.

"Oh no!" she gasped. Her eyes went wide. You'd have thought I'd parked a rusty truck piled high with refuse on her lawn.

She shuddered and shook her head. "Well! Can

we get this over with quickly, please? My guests will arrive soon," she bristled.

Her eyes came back to me. She looked at my hat, settled briefly on my badge and then dropped down to my black boots. Size 14.

Some fellows who preferred to look over their shoulders rather than just follow state fishing and hunting regulations called me "Bigfoot."

Her eyebrows shot up. She looked over her shoulder to study her entryway. I had noticed it right off. It was a mosaic of highly polished, exotic woods. Very nice.

She turned back to me, and with a thin lipped smile, said, "I think it best if you walk up the driveway and meet me out back."

She began to shut the door in my face and added, "Thank you," just before she slammed it shut.

I read somewhere that Eleanor Roosevelt said, "No one can make you feel inferior without your permission." It struck me Mrs. Roosevelt must have run into some of this woman's relatives.

I stood there looking at the closed castle door, took a deep breath, turned around, walked down the granite steps and up the driveway to the back of the house.

There was a big sunroom there, with a wall of open windows and fresh white curtains trembling in the gentle morning breeze.

It was clear this was where the real living went on. It was a lovely, sunny spot.

Through the glass, I saw two big bouquets of flowers set atop a linen tablecloth and heard someone moving around inside.

It looked like one or two people in black and white uniforms were setting a long table with plates, glasses and silverware.

The homeowner appeared in the patio door. She stepped out onto a wide step made of bricks, crossed her arms and began to tell me more about her problem.

"It has been walking through the yard almost every day early in the morning or late at night," she said with disgust. "My husband and I are like prisoners here. We have to keep watch for the... that animal! We aren't even safe in our own home!"

"Do you leave any food or garbage out, Ma'am?" I asked her.

"Certainly NOT!" she said emphatically. "Our housekeeper takes the trash with her. She puts it in a container the community uses."

I continued, "Is anyone feeding any feral cats? Skunks love cat food."

When I said "skunk" she shuddered. Her eyes rolled up into the back of her head and her right hand went to her forehead like she was a star in an old Hollywood movie, about to faint.

When she recovered, she opened her eyes and explained, "There are no dogs or cats roaming here. We have rules! Dogs must be leashed and with a person when they go outside. As for cats, if anyone has one, they would be indoors only. Animals are certainly not allowed to roam here."

"Well, Ma'am, your development is surrounded by woods and wild animals do travel," I reminded her. "This is Vermont."

She stood before me grimacing and crossed her arms. For a few seconds there was silence between us.

And that's when we both heard it.

There was a rustling outside the sunroom, maybe 25 feet away from my left shoulder. It was coming from the greenery that hid the foundation.

"Oh no! It's him!" she hissed with a mixture of outrage and disgust. "It's that animal!! He's back in my azaleas!"

I put my fingers to my lips, to signal her to be quiet, stepped back about 10 feet and listened.

I heard more scratching and dirt being thrown up against something, maybe lattice work along the bottom of the sunporch.

"He's in there! Oh! Oh! Oh! Get it out of here! DO SOMETHING!" she hissed at me. Her long fingers with their bright nail polish clutched her cheeks, her heels lifted out of her shoes.

"My guests will be here in a half hour! Nancy is setting the table now. I can't have it here. I can't have it! That animal, and you, need to be gone before they arrive!" she said.

I nodded, to let her know I was listening to her as I walked quietly, parallel to her patio and about 20 feet away from the greenery there. I bent down every couple of strides and peered beneath the trunks of the perfectly trimmed gumdrop yews and flowering shrubs.

She came off the steps to watch me.

In a few long, slow strides, I spotted a blotch of white and black fur tucked just behind some sturdy yews.

It was a skunk all right and he was digging hard, after something.

Whether he was trying to get himself some lunch or he just wanted to get under the lattice so he could crawl under the porch for a cool summer snooze, I didn't know.

I stood up and looked back at the woman.

If it was someone else, I would have suggested she move her party from the sunroom to elsewhere in the house. A live trap could be set and he'd be caught and removed in a day or two.

Problem solved, if there was just one of them.

But she had made it very clear the animal had to go immediately. She didn't appear open to any other ideas.

I'd had a pretty good rapport with skunks over the years. I'd even removed young skunks from window wells at Porter Hospital. I'd just approach them quietly, drop a cloth over them, pick them up gently and carry them off. If you go slow enough, don't talk, you can often move them without triggering their defensive spray.

But I could tell this skunk was no baby. It was full grown. And it was already agitated a little. Who knows what the homeowners had been doing to attempt to get it to leave?

I had to approach this one more cautiously.

"I'll be right back, Ma'am," I told her and I headed to my truck.

In the back was a telescoping pole, basically a boat hook. I thought maybe I could use it to get beneath the hedge and gently urge the skunk to move along before her guests arrived.

She could have her party and none of them would know she had a potential party crasher outside. Later, I could give her some ideas for skunk proofing her place.

I grabbed the pole from my truck and trotted back to the edge of the patio, slowing when I approached the hedge perimeter. I listened.

The lady of the house was back up on the top step, in the open doorway, talking to the people getting her home ready for the party.

She stood there glaring at me, biting her lip and

tapping a toe as I bent down to determine the best way to get the pole near the skunk.

I saw her glance at her wristwatch. "Hurry!!" she pleaded.

I sidled up closer to the greenery, bent down and pushed the pole atop a layer of mulch, between some yews and a couple azaleas, in a straight line.

My plan was to wiggle the pole just a tiny bit, so the skunk would raise his head, maybe think a snake was near him and leave.

It was tough getting through the plantings because the pole wouldn't bend. I didn't want to be in a straight line looking at the skunk, in case he bolted.

I managed to get it within six feet of him. I got my eyes down low, waited for him to take a break from his digging and shook my end a little so the sound would telegraph down to him.

No go. The skunk ignored me.

I moved closer, stuck my arm in as far as it would go beneath the shrubbery, swung the handle harder, knocking the trunks of the bushes a few feet from the skunk.

The metal pole clunked against the woody stems.

He stopped digging and lifted his head, trying to figure out what was making the sound. His nose went way up in the air, sniffing the breeze.

He was trying to see, smell, and hear if a threat was approaching.

I stopped shaking the pole and froze. I hoped he would decide it was time to leave.

But after 15 seconds, he lowered his head again. The hair on his back laid flat and he went back to nosing around at the ground and resumed digging.

From inside the patio, I heard furniture being dragged across the floor, lots of talk and heavy footsteps.

I was concerned all the hustle and bustle inside the sunroom, on the other side of those open windows, might set this skunk off.

You just never know. Skunks march to their own drummer. They don't like to be pushed or prodded or told what to do.

"Aren't you done yet?" The woman called out the door. "My guests will be here in just a few minutes!"

I wanted to help her. It was do or die time.

I extended the pole again, got it to within a foot
of where the skunk was hunched over digging.
I shook the handle hard, back and forth. I wanted
the yew bushes to shake, to prompt him to pick
up his head and scurry off.

And it could have worked. It should have worked.
But with the slamming and snapping and tinkling
coming from up above him inside the patio, and
the lady of the house shouting at me and the yews
shaking, I guess it all became too much for him.

The skunk stopped digging, threw up his head
and skittered out of the bushes onto the back
lawn in three skunky bounds.

He stood just six feet from all those pretty
starched white curtains inside the open windows.

He planted his front feet, lifted his tail straight
up in the air – the black and white hair spread
nearly a foot wide – almost like a wild tom turkey
fanning his tail.

Plates hit the tables inside, silverware clanged
and clinked. Feet stomped and ran on the
floorboards. And hearing all that noise, that's

where he aimed his fabled furry flag.

His backside pointed at the curtains dancing in
the light morning breeze, at all that noise.

And with a "Hi Ho Silver! Away!" he told everyone
what he thought of those who would deter him
from walking and hunting for a meal on the land
of his ancestors.

There was nothing I could do.

It was a direct hit. The breeze lifted the eye
watering stench up and over the shrubbery
into the festive sunroom, carried it deep into
the house. It rolled on towards my truck in the
driveway and all of the neighbors.

I scrambled to my feet and took off upwind as fast
as I could.

I looked over at the homeowner. Her eyes went as
wide as cue balls. Her hands flew to her cheeks.

She screamed, turned and darted inside the patio
door, which slammed behind her.

She was like a woman whose house is on fire
but runs back inside to save the china. She
would have been better off running away from
the stink. But there was no way to tell her this.

She was gone.

I heard her yelling, "Nancy! Shut the door! Shut the windows! Nancy! Nancyyyyyyy!!" from inside the house. But I knew from experience, there was nothing anyone could do.

The skunk had spoken.

I was on my feet, glaring at him as he began to lower his tail after the blast.

I knew the lady's entire house and a lot of her neighbors would be sniffing skunk for a week, maybe two.

The little stinkers pack a punch.

I shook my head, shortened my pole a bit, then swatted the ground with the end about six feet behind the stinker and said, "Shoo! Go on. Get out of here! And keep going!"

The skunk loped off into the woods adjoining the backyard and disappeared.

I shook my head, picked up my pole, slid the pieces inside each other and walked to my truck. As I came in line with the home's sun porch I got the full stink bomb. My eyes began to water, my mouth tasted skunky.

Walking beside the house, I heard more yelling
and screeching and wailing. Windows and doors
were being slammed all over the castle.

I knew there was no point in knocking on the front
door and attempting to speak with the owner.

She would be calling her guests telling them
to stay away, then leaping out of her high heels
and bangles, wriggling out of her tight dress and
jumping into a long hot shower while working on
a plan to deskunk her home.

I dropped the pole into the back of my truck,
climbed inside the cab, turned on the ignition and
headed home.

Whether the skunk took my advice and stayed
gone or it returned and the lady called some pest
control outfit to handle him, I don't know.

I only know she never called me again for help.

"His shot struck the tree less than two feet
from my head. Shards of bark and
frozen sap blew into my face as the
bullet bit deep into the heartwood."

IAN

CONTRIBUTED BY JOHN KAPUSTA

If you think being a game warden is all fun and games, well... you probably shouldn't read this story. There's more suspense than laughs.

But it happened.

And some of us wardens think readers need to be reminded now and again that we deal with some very tough characters. Ian was one of mine.

When you're responsible for putting a man in prison – not once, but twice – for two to three years each time – you can pretty much guess what he thinks of you.

And we all know some guys will boast to their buddies, "That so and so who put me away? I'm gonna make him pay..." over a few beers.

Still, it is rare for a guy to actually act on his revenge fantasy. After all, it's a sure ticket to put him back behind bars, whether he's successful or not.

But Ian? He was different. Ian really didn't like being told what to do.

He tried to kill me. And not just once. He really wanted me gone.

But I guess I should start at the beginning.

It was a week before deer rifle season. Everybody who was planning to be out hunting on opening day was gearing up. Serious hunters had already spent hours in the woods looking for deer sign and plotting where the best spot would be when they entered the woods before sunrise on opening day.

And when deer hunters who follow the rules suspect somebody else isn't – suspect somebody is poaching deer – they don't like it at all. That's how this all started.

I got a call around 8 a.m. from a fellow saying gunshots had been fired the night before. He believed the shots had come from a neighbor's property, a guy who owned a couple hundred acres way out on a dirt road, in a town most Vermonters will never visit.

This caller said it wasn't the first time he'd heard it. There was a lot of shooting going on at night. He couldn't be certain, but he thought he knew who was doing it.

"What's the fellow's name?" I asked him.

"Ian McLeod," he said.

There was little doubt in my mind the shooting meant someone was poaching deer. But before I drove over to have a chat, I ran a background check on Mr. McLeod.

I learned he was 43 years old and a convicted felon – burglary and multiple assaults. Now, I knew he had a temper. As I read down the list, I saw some of the cases were only a couple of years old.

That told me it wasn't like he'd made mistakes when he was younger and then straightened out. Nope, this fellow hadn't calmed down. It was the way he lived his life.

All those felonies made his owning or possessing any gun illegal.

So, Ian could land himself back in jail if I saw him with a firearm or they were in his home. The law was clear.

I drove over to his place to introduce myself later that same morning.

Ian's property was a former dairy farm set back on a long private driveway off a sparsely

populated – by humans, anyway – dirt road.
The milkers were gone and a field I figured had
been used for pasture was sporting junipers five
and eight feet tall.

I rolled slowly down his winding dirt driveway
taking in the lay of the land, house and barns.
And I made note the land was not posted
against anyone trespassing – in case I might
want to return.

I saw four or five vehicles parked near the
house, two of them sporting license plates from
Rhode Island. That told me Ian was not alone
and I should be extra careful when I knocked
on his door.

I parked in the driveway, opened my door and
heard multiple male voices shouting over loud
music booming inside the home 40 feet away.

I figured they wouldn't have heard me pull up
with the music that loud.

I had just set foot on the farmhouse porch when
the front door flew open and a fellow came
charging out, slamming the door shut behind him.

He came at me fast, stopped four feet away and
snarled, "What do you want?"

He was wearing a worn brown canvas farm coat with a shearling lining beneath. The jacket had big, deep pockets for carrying tools. It was loose enough to make me wonder if he might have a pistol tucked inside.

"I'm Vermont Fish and Game Warden John Kapusta," I said calmly. "I'm here because I've had a complaint about guns being fired at night on this road. Are you the homeowner, Ian McLeod?"

I was maybe an arm's length away from him, with my eyes on his face. But his hands concerned me most. They were low, elbows cocked a little, his body almost trembling with rage. I saw him curl his fingers into fists, his knuckles going from tan to white.

"Yes," he said.

"Do you know anything about shooting at night?" I asked him.

"No!" he growled, "I don't. I haven't heard anything," he added, glaring at me. "Some of the people around here," he shouted while looking off down his drive, "They just want to cause trouble."

He shook his head in disgust, took a deep breath and looked hard at me, like he was sizing me up.

He and I were about the same height and weight. I could see that under his coat he had broad shoulders. He looked rugged and he was acting like a man unafraid to fight.

"Is that it then?" he demanded. "You got a search warrant?"

"No warrant," I said. "I'm just visiting and talking to neighbors, making certain there's no shooting at night, no poaching going on."

Ian shifted his balance from heel to toe, like a boxer standing in his corner, preparing for the bell to ring.

"Well, there's nothing going on here," he said, leaning into me a couple inches and biting the end off each word.

I didn't back up. He didn't like that I held my ground.

"So, how about you just leave?" Ian said, raising his chin in defiance.

"Call me if you hear anything," I replied. Then I nodded, turned and walked back to my cruiser.

I listened for the porch door opening and shutting behind me, or his feet running across the porch after me. But he didn't do either.

The only sound was my boots down the steps and across the gravel to my car. That meant he was still on the porch, watching me.

I turned my cruiser around and slowly headed down his driveway, pulling out a pen and paper and scribbling the Rhode Island license plate numbers down as I drove. I took in the lay of the house, barn and land, without being obvious about it.

Just before I rounded a bend, I looked back in my rear view mirror. I saw Ian was still there on the porch – arms crossed, watching me and scowling.

I drove away knowing a couple things. Ian was now on notice he was a suspect. I'd be back and he knew it.

And Ian had made his point. He didn't like law enforcement. That meant he didn't like me and he did not want me on his property.

Most guys will quit jacking deer once the warden comes around asking questions – at least for a little while.

They wait a couple weeks, and when they figure the warden has moved on to other cases, forgotten about them, they start up again.

But Ian apparently could not wait. And he had bigger ideas than killing deer.

A week later, the phone rang and when I picked it up, I heard a voice I recognized. It was one of my "CIs" – short for confidential informant. I had cited him into court several times for hunting and fishing violations.

He still hung out with fellows who liked to break the law now and again, even if he pretty much kept his nose clean. He'd given me good information on several occasions in the past and I trusted him, up to a point.

Sometimes you need the fellows on the inside of poaching rings. These guys are often willing to turn in somebody they don't like.

"Kapusta, I'm calling to warn you," this fellow said quietly. "I was in a bar the other night with Ian and his Rhode Island buddies. We were all drinking. They said you'd stopped by a few days earlier."

"Oh?" I said. I wanted him to know I was still listening, but not give him any information. Still, the fact he knew I'd been at Ian's said something.

"That crowd does a lot of night hunting over there. The bunch of them said they don't want you interfering with their plans. Ian and his pals came up with a plan to get rid of you."

"Really?" I said, wanting him to tell me more. He might be telling me the truth. But he might also be part of the set up. I knew he played both sides. I wasn't about to tell him anything.

"Hunh," I added calmly, just to let him know I was still on the line.

"Look! This ain't no idle chit chat," he hissed into the phone. "These guys are serious! Ian's friends from Rhode Island are bad dudes, real bad. I'm pretty certain they've killed people before. And now, they've got a plan to get you."

"Well, what is it?" I asked him.

"They are gonna get you to come over to Ian's, make up some complaint, then jump you from behind and tie you to an apple tree."

"And then what?" I asked.

He took a deep breath. I could hear him practically squirming on the other end of the line. He didn't want to say it out loud.

"They said they are gonna get a big knife and," he stopped right there.

I waited. When he didn't finish his sentence, I spoke calmly, "And what?"

I heard him take another deep breath. Then he spoke fast, like the words had stuck in his head, but he wished they hadn't.

"They said they would get a big knife and spill your guts out on the ground."

"Hunh," I said, again not showing emotion, just encouraging him to tell me more.

The CI didn't appreciate my monotone responses.

"Kapusta! Wake up! They're really going to do it!!" he shouted into the phone – so loud I had to pull the receiver three inches from my ear.

"This ain't a joke! They were going over the plan, finalizing it last night. I was right there," he said, trying to impress upon me the seriousness of the threat.

He was riled up. I held my tongue and let him go.

"Ian, he said he doesn't want anyone bothering him, telling him what to do. He said he has got to get rid of you. And the others, those Rhode Island guys, they told Ian they'd help him do it."

"Un hunh," I said.

He continued, "Look, you know me. I don't mind bendin' a few fishin' and huntin' laws now and again, but this is..." He stopped again. I could tell he was searching for the right words.

"Well, it's nuthin' I want to be involved with," he said.

"I'm only calling because I couldn't live with myself if you ended up dead and I hadn't at least called to warn you."

"When is this going to happen?" I asked him.

"I don't know exactly, but soon. Soon," he said.

All the time I was listening to the CI, I was hatching a plan. I wasn't certain this fellow was telling me the truth. He played both sides. If there was a plot to kill me, how could I know for sure this fellow wasn't part of it?

Maybe he was just pretending to help me out? Maybe the whole idea was to get me more interested, to get me over there.

But it didn't matter. I was pretty certain there was poaching going on over at Ian's. I had a duty to stop him if he was deer jacking.

"So, how do they do their poaching?" I asked.

"Ian planted some deer feed," he told me. "He's got several plots. And there's some apple trees too. He goes out after midnight a few nights a week, follows a trail."

"There's a routine?" I asked.

"Oh yeah. Some of his land sits on an old quarry. There's a railroad that used to run through part of it, where they'd carry the stone to the mill. The track is gone, but that's what he uses. He walks that old rail line."

"Does he leave from a back door or what?" I asked, trying to learn as much as I could.

"He always heads counter clockwise off the front porch. He makes a big circle. It takes him about an hour – maybe a little longer if he comes back with a deer."

"What time does he head out?" I asked him.

"Most of the time, midnight or later," he said. "But sometimes he'll head out a couple hours earlier. Just depends on his mood."

I was thinking to myself, "It's clear this fellow has spent time at Ian's. They must trust him. You don't plan a murder in front of just anyone. If I'm going to stop Ian, I need this CI with me. I need to know what he knows."

"I need to see what you are talking about," I told him. "I want you come with me, at night, and show me. Will you do that?"

The line went dead for a few seconds. I waited.

I heard a sputter, followed by a deep sigh.

He finally said, "If that's what it's gonna take so no one gets hurt, yes, I'll go. But I don't want them seeing me. They can't know I tipped you off. They'll kill me too."

"Don't worry," I assured him. "They'll never even know we were there. I just want to look."

He sighed again and said, "When?"

Thanksgiving was two days away. I told him to meet me Thursday night, at 8 p.m. on a back road in a neighboring town. I'd drive an unmarked car and dress in civilian clothes. I gave him the make of the car and the license plate number.

"Weatherman says it's going to be really cold all week, so dress for the weather," I added. "We could be standing and watching awhile. And there's probably more than a foot of snow up at his place."

"I got it. I'll be there," he said and hung up the phone.

I dug out my notes, where I had written down the license plate numbers of Ian's friends. It was time to check them out too.

I called into the office to get the vehicle registrations and then ask about the criminal background of the owners.

Ian's pals made him look like a choirboy. They'd each spent many years behind bars. One of them had been convicted of manslaughter.

It was another indication what the CI told me might actually be true.

I called my neighboring warden, Ron Gonyaw, and told him a little of what I was looking into. Ron offered to come with me. I thanked him, but told him not this time. I'd call if I needed his help.

The family and I had Thanksgiving dinner around 5 p.m. and with the dishes almost dry and put

away and football games taking over the TV,
I quietly told the wife I had to go to work.

She pursed her lips, nodded and forced a
small smile.

I knew she would have preferred for me to stay
home, read a bedtime story to the kids, chat
with her and relax. It would be nice to spend an
entire holiday at home. But I'd told her before we
married there was no holiday, no family occasion I
would put before my duty to uphold the law.

I pulled on two pairs of socks and my insulated
boots. When I reached for a warm winter hat,
she followed me to the door and gave me a
goodbye kiss.

"No uniform?" she asked.

"Just going to take a look," I said and smiled.

Then I added like it was just an afterthought, "If
I'm not here when you get up in the morning, call
Ron Gonyaw. He'll know where to find me."

I didn't say anything more. I didn't want to worry
her. Was I supposed to tell her I was going to
scope out my upcoming murder?

"Should I be worried?" she asked me.

"Nah," I said, and smiled.

Usually I would take a deputy with me or a warden, but not this time. And there were a couple of reasons for that.

I didn't want to put anyone else in danger. And I didn't want to spook my informant. He made it clear he didn't want anyone to know he was helping me.

The voice inside my head told me this was the way to go. If what the CI said was true, there was no telling what these guys were capable of.

The CI showed up on time Thanksgiving night, jumped into my passenger seat and said, "Listen. Why don't you just ask me what you want to know and go there by yourself?"

"Because once I'm there, I'll have more questions," I told him. "We'll be fine. Let's go," I said, and threw my car into reverse so he'd be less likely to leave. "We'll walk off a bit of our big dinners, right?"

I wasn't going to give him the chance to back out. I got out on the road, drove to within a half mile of Ian's and pulled my car up a driveway to an unoccupied summer camp. I knew no one would see it from the road, especially this night.

216

Everyone was home recovering from feasting with family and watching football or some special on TV. Who would expect anyone wearing a badge to be out working?

When we entered Ian's property I carried binoculars and, for added insurance against the cold, I had a padded throw with me, the kind moving companies use to protect furniture. It was bulky, but I found them to be great at keeping me warm.

This one was solid green on one side and brown on the other, good enough to blend into most wooded areas on a long night of surveillance.

I carried my sidearm under my coat, but no rifle. I wanted to be able to move silently through the woods. I didn't want to risk having anyone hear steel tick a tree branch or worse, get caught if I had to run for it.

It was a moonless night, well below zero, with a foot of snow on the ground.

I didn't like that we would leave boot prints behind, but there wasn't anything we could do about that.

Walking through snow was quieter than through dead leaves. And where I planned to be that

night – up above Ian's house looking down and
in through his windows – I didn't figure anyone
would be checking for intruders anyhow.

But it was so very cold, the snow squeaked with
every step. The sound of leather and rubber
compressing snow carries a long ways. I knew
we might be heard up to 50 feet away if someone
was outside. A guy standing outside having a
cigarette, taking a dog for a late night walk or yes,
night hunting?

If we were heard and forced to run, this cold,
silent night and easy tracking could get my CI
and me killed.

I didn't say anything to my already reluctant
partner about it. But I knew we had to be extra
careful. We couldn't make any noise as we edged
close to the house.

While walking through the woods to the knoll
above Ian's we didn't speak, other than an
occasional whisper. "Watch out for that stump,"
and "Stay low."

I had made a point of not telling the CI where I
intended to set up on Ian. If the crew planned
on rushing me, I didn't want to show my hand.
I wasn't 100 percent convinced my informant was
being honest with me.

It didn't take long for us to reach the spot I had chosen, a wooded plateau above Ian's house. Just inside the maple and fir stand, my informant and I each took cover. Each of us snugged our bodies against wide trees 10 feet or so into the tree line, looking down and into the house. We were probably 250 feet away.

I was concerned about getting too close to the house. There were mixed court rulings on an issue called "curtilage." It was all about how close law officers could get to a residence or other location when conducting surveillance. The law was not settled on this issue.

Even though I wasn't planning to act this night – just watch – I didn't want to do anything that might get the case I hoped to bring later, tossed out.

I raised my binoculars and studied the house. The lights from inside cast light out onto the porch and a few feet beyond, into the yard.

I could hear faint music coming up the hill. It sounded like people inside were having a party. And now and again I would hear poplar leaves gently rustling above our heads in the treetops.

I counted four fellows, each of them holding a glass or a beer bottle in their hand. It looked like they were playing cards or some sort of game.

But what I wanted to see what they had for firearms. And I couldn't see any from my spot atop the knoll.

I opened the quilt I'd brought, carefully wrapped it around my shoulders and leaned on a stout tree to help steady my glasses, hoping they'd go hunting.

The CI stood off to my right and behind me about five feet away. We waited.

There were cars and trucks parked off to the right, in the shadows of the house. I couldn't see them clearly, but their shape was similar to the vehicles I'd seen parked in Ian's yard when he and I met. That told me the same friends were likely in there with him.

We stood there an hour, then close to two, just watching and listening. The cold settled deeper. And still no one left the house.

The CI crept slowly over to me and whispered, "It shouldn't be long now. When they come out of the house, they'll head counterclockwise."

But I had my doubts. It felt more like January than November. And if they'd feasted on turkey, stuffing, potatoes, pies, watched hours of football and maybe been drinking alcohol, would they really feel like going hunting?

I waited another 20 minutes. Finally, I couldn't take it any longer. I needed to know how many guys we were talking about and what kind of weapons they had in the house. I'd never see either one from where I stood.

I motioned for the CI to come over to me, then whispered, "I want to get closer. Let's head down to the old dairy barn."

The CI nodded.

"You know the layout. You go first and I'll follow. Stay low and in the shadows. If we get separated, get into that cow barn. I'll meet you there."

I had him go first so I'd be safer in case he was intending to double cross me. I watched as he ducked low, scooted through the trees, crossed the open area between the woods and ducked alongside the barn not far from the house.

As soon as he was safely near the house, I took a deep breath, pulled the quilt tighter around my neck and shoulders, and ran after him.

I made it maybe 200 feet – in the weeds just off

the driveway – when the front door opened and
a guy holding a bright light stepped out onto the
porch. He began sweeping the yard in front of the
house with it.

I threw myself face down into the snow and pulled
the quilt up over my back. I was like a three year
old hiding from the bogeyman under the covers.
Only this bogeyman was real and I didn't close
my eyes. I wanted to see what – if anything
– was coming.

I lay with my face down in the snow, not moving a
muscle, wondering if my boot heels were sticking
out, wondering if the fellow with the light had
seen me, wondering what the spotlight would tell
him when it swept over me.

I was afraid the jig was up. If his light threw a
bright beam 100 yards, enough for them to see
a human figure lying under this mover's quilt,
I figured I'd be killed. I hoped they'd bought a
cheap light.

I listened for footsteps, for voices. I wanted to
reach for my revolver, but I didn't dare move a
muscle. It would be no match for a man with a
rifle anyhow.

I felt like a rabbit in winter that had strayed too
far from its den. A brown quilted rectangle lying

in the snow? Fresh prints leading to it? If Ian
saw it...

Unlike the rabbit, I knew what came next. I could
be shot dead, never having had a chance to
defend myself.

Some hunters who find the rabbit sitting still in
plain sight, hiding, they smile and hold the barrel
two inches from the rabbit's head, shoot and call
that sporting. Others will stamp their foot next to
the animal, forcing it to run and then shoot.

I was hoping this fellow – whoever he was – would
do that for me. Let me get to my feet and make a
run for it. I didn't want to die this way.

I saw the night lighten to dusk as the beam swept
from the porch through the yard, over and across
the driveway.

For all I knew the fellow coursing the light
through the yard had a friend leaning on an open
windowsill – a rifle barrel resting there – just
waiting to take a shot. The marksman could stay
warm and his aim would be more accurate.

The snow in front of my eyes brightened.

I listened. Would I hear them put a bullet in the
chamber? Click the safety off?

I didn't feel the cold. I didn't feel anything. I tried to control my breathing and just listen. I realized the decision on whether I lived or died wasn't mine anymore.

Four seconds later, the snow in front of my eyes went black again. The beam headed towards the barn. I lay in darkness, waiting.

I stayed still. A flick of the wrist would be all it took to bring that light back onto my quilt. But if what the fellow saw didn't register as human, I might still get away.

A few seconds later, I heard footsteps – someone walking on the porch – followed by the screen door hinges creaking and the door slapping the jamb.

When I heard the door slam shut, I knew it was now or never.

I leaped to my feet, stayed low and ran – the quilt trailing me like a comet. I headed towards the dairy barn 80 feet away.

There was no question in my mind the fellow with the light had seen something lying in the distance. Whether he realized there was a person lying face down under the thick quilt or not, he had to know something was out of place. He was probably telling the others what he saw right now.

I had to get to the CI before a crowd came storming out of the house and bullets flew.

Running towards the barn meant heading closer to the house. But I had no choice. I was not going to leave my informant behind.

I slid through the barn door and saw the CI's shadow. He was inside waiting for me.

"They saw me," I hissed. "We gotta run for it. Meet me back on the hill. Go!"

The CI scrambled for the exit like a mouse surprised by a cat on a freshly waxed kitchen floor. I let him go first, then backed out the door, the quilt bunched under one arm. I stayed in the shadows and ran for the woods.

We each made a wide sweep away from the cow barn, dove into the tree line and climbed up the back of the ridge to the hilltop.

Fifteen minutes later, we found each other on the knoll.

"I don't like this," the fellow whispered while trying to catching his breath. "I don't like this at all. Come on, Kapusta. We gotta get outta here!"

"It'll be all right," I said quietly to calm him.

"They'll figure whoever they saw has left in a big hurry. They've got no idea where we are right now. I just want to watch them a little longer and see what they do."

I folded my quilt and put it behind me, then walked back to the widest tree, and continued to watch the house through my binoculars.

Five minutes later, the front door opened and a man came out dressed for the weather – hat pulled down low and a scarf across his face, holding a rifle in his arms.

A second man followed, wearing a heavy coat, hat and mittens and carrying a flashlight.

They stood side by side, talking to one another.

Inside the house, the music was still playing. Whether the cold night air was making the noise carry farther, I don't know. But the music seemed louder than before.

Whatever they thought they had seen earlier, it hadn't stopped the party.

The fellow with the flashlight turned it on and moved the beam around the yard. He started off to his right, swept left slowly. Then he went back, raising his light up a bit higher and repeated the

sweep slowly over the hill. He was methodical.
The light went back and forth like a pendulum.

I let the quilt fall to the ground from my
shoulders, pasted myself to the side of the tree
so we would appear as one, then raised my
binoculars again to get a better look.

The fellow holding the rifle was wearing a
coat like I had seen Ian wear when I'd met him.
And the way he stood? Feet wide apart, planted
and proud, chin up, ready for a fight?

Even with the scarf across his face like a bank
robber, I was 99 percent certain that man was Ian.

The beam came higher, swept across the hill
where my CI and I were standing. I dropped
my binoculars and slammed my side against
the tree, my arms and hands flat against my
sides. I wanted to blend in with the tree and
keep watching.

The CI was off to my right, maybe 15 feet and
standing another 10 feet deeper in the trees, out
of sight.

Had the fellows down below spotted us? The light
didn't stop. It moved on. I figured we were good.

But we weren't.

The fellow with the spotlight let the beam drop
to his side. He tilted his head, raised his arm,
pointed up at the hill and said something to Ian.
I stood still, just watching them.

Ian nodded, lifted the gun to his shoulder, aimed
quickly and fired.

His shot struck the tree less than two feet from
my head. Shards of bark and frozen sap blew into
my face as the bullet bit deep into the heartwood.

I spun around to the back of the trunk, bent my
shoulders and arms in tight and froze. I was
trying to make myself as narrow as possible in
case the shooter wasn't done.

I waited knowing I was trapped.

Ian took his time. He aimed up into the
hillside and fired, paused, aimed again and
fired. And then again.

Three more bullets ripped by me into the woods,
all of them not more than a few feet away from
where I was hiding.

This wasn't random shooting. This was a man
shooting to kill.

I peered into the dark, tried to see or hear my

informant. Had he been hit? Where was he?
Had he dropped down into the snow to avoid
being shot? Or had he run off to join Ian's crew?
Was this all part of my being set up? Was I about
to be ambushed?

I listened and waited another 20 seconds.

I saw something – a shadow in the shape of a
man. He was making tracks away from the
house, headed off the hill.

It was my informant headed back to the car. I took
a chance, stuck my head out from behind the tree
and looked over my left shoulder at the house.

I saw the guy with the spotlight had shut it off
and the second man – the one I believed to be
Ian – had dropped the rifle's muzzle to just below
his knees.

Maybe they figured they had made their point?
Or maybe the rifle was silent because Ian had
sent a few of his pals to circle around to see if one
of the bullets had found me?

Was my informant disappearing part of their plan?

I didn't know exactly what was going on. I only
knew I had to get out of there. I ran for it, hoping
I wasn't inviting a bullet in the back or someone

hiding in the woods ahead of me waiting to kill me.

I hurried through the snow, across the hill, back towards the town road. I stopped now and again, to listen for the sound of boots in snow coming at me.

There was only the sound of my breath in the freezing night air.

When I intersected the town road, I stayed in the tree line. I didn't show myself. I didn't want to take the chance of a vehicle carrying Ian or his pals coming up on me fast and finding me in the road.

When I reached the car, I found my CI waiting for me.

Despite the bitter cold, I could tell he was steaming. We didn't speak until we climbed into the front seat and quietly shut the car doors.

Then, as soon as he could get his breath, he growled, "I told you these guys weren't kidding. You want to get yourself killed, Kapusta? You go ahead. But I'm done. Done!"

He took a deep breath, shook his head, leaned back against the seat, closed his eyes and added, "Just take me back to my car."

I didn't try to talk him into reconsidering or ask him more questions. I did what he asked. I turned on the car and backed onto the town road.

The quiet gave me time to come up with my next move. But before the CI exited my car, I said, "Thank you for your help." Maybe some of his anger had left. He said, "Good luck," before he left me alone.

I looked at my watch and saw it was still early. There was plenty of night left. It was another opportunity. I didn't feel close to being done with watching Ian and his crew.

I drove home, knocked the snow off my boots, walked into the house, picked up the phone and called Ron.

"Ron, I know it's Thanksgiving, but I wondered if you could help me out tonight," I said. "No need for the uniform. Surveillance only. Just dress warm. It's cold out there."

Ron immediately agreed and said he could meet me within the hour.

I didn't say anything more on the phone, because I didn't want my wife hearing how she came awful close to being a widow a little earlier. I'd explain things to Ron when we met.

231

I was certain Ian and his pals would think they had run me off. They'd believe I had hightailed it and was running scared.

They'd never expect me to come right back. And that meant they would let their guard down, maybe even be so bold as to go night hunting. And that's what I needed to see, to build a case against them.

With Ron by my side, I'd have a witness who could also testify against them.

And if I got myself hurt or killed, Ron would make certain things were taken care of there too.

It wasn't long before Ron and I were back on the same hill where I had stood with the CI earlier in the night. Only I had us set up a lot farther down the ridge. I figured they might still be looking at where I'd been standing.

The lights were bright in the house and the music was cranked up three times louder. The "boom boom boom" of the bass literally rattled the windows at times.

I figured that was a sign the party was really rolling now. What else would they do to celebrate?

Ron and I didn't have to wait long.

We saw the front door open. Two fellows came outside, dressed in heavy hunting coats and wearing gloves. The fellow I believed was Ian again held a firearm. But it had a shorter barrel than what he had been holding earlier. Held tight against his coat, the light at the men's backs, it was hard to make out just what it was.

We watched as the two of them consulted for a bit, both of them weaving a little and looking down at the rifle.

Ian raised the muzzle up towards the woods – to the left of where Ron and I were watching – and pulled the trigger.

"Rat a tat a tat a tat a tat!" the weapon blasted up into the hill, 500 feet away from where Ron and I were hidden. Ian was pushed back on his heels by the gun. He fired probably 60 rounds in just a few seconds.

I'd taught firearms courses for years. This was no hunting rifle. It was an AK 47, a weapon of war. And while it was legal to own one that had been modified – if you weren't a convicted felon – it was illegal to own one that fired continually with a single trigger pull. This AK 47 was illegal. Someone had changed it back.

And since the fellow shooting was Ian, a convicted

felon, the violation was worse.

Ron and I hunkered down and waited.

Over the next couple hours, fellows walked in and out of the farmhouse, some with bottles in their hands or a glass. They took turns, blistering the trees above the house with hundreds of bullets from the AK 47.

The good news was, they didn't shoot anywhere close to where Ron and I were hidden.

Around 3 a.m., the music stopped. We saw lights go off in the front of the house and some turned on in the second story. Bedrooms, I figured. That told us they were done for the night.

We waited a few more minutes, then dropped back off the hill and hiked out of the woods to my car.

I was disappointed no one had gone deer hunting that night. But it was pretty clear Ian was after bigger game – me.

I thanked Ron and said I'd be in touch. I needed to get warm and catch some sleep, then make my next move.

Right after the long holiday weekend, I called the federal Bureau of Alcohol, Tobacco and Firearms

– the ATF. The agency is responsible for enforcing the law when it comes to felons possessing firearms. I may not have seen Ian hunting, but I sure saw him shooting.

When officials learned there was an automatic weapon in the hands of a convicted felon, that really got their attention.

In a matter of days, the ATF raided Ian's home and he landed himself back in prison. After a trial, he received a two year sentence.

I figured he'd do his time and when he got out, his fascination with steel and gunpowder would be over. He'd have moved on.

But not long after Ian's release from prison, my phone rang again with complaints from neighbors. It was the same problem and same time of year – shots in the night over at Ian's, right around deer season.

I knew it would do no good to pay the man a visit and have another talk.

He'd had 24 hours a day for two years to come up with another hobby that didn't involve guns – fishing, boating, racing cars, rock climbing – you name it. But if what neighbors said was true, Ian – or someone in his house – was breaking the law again.

And if he was poaching deer, it was my job to stop him. I didn't like the idea of just calling the ATF again. I had a deer herd to protect as well as the rights of other hunters who purchased licenses and hunted lawfully.

And it might not be Ian. It could be some of his buddies. But whoever was night hunting over at his place, I intended to stop them.

I recalled what the CI had told me, about the rail line and the men always walking it counterclockwise. I wanted to see it for myself, to get the layout of the trail they used, see the food plots, buildings and woods.

Where were these deer being cut up? Where did Ian dispose of the bones and hides? Were his friends taking venison, maybe selling the meat down in Rhode Island? How big an operation was this? What exactly was going on?

I decided to head back over to Ian's place at night, walk the trail and see for myself.

I knew if he found me there, he'd likely try to kill me again. But I had to know more.

My deputies offered to come with me. They urged

me to take them along or at least one of them.

I said no. I didn't want to expose other fellows to the danger of being shot or killed. Not yet anyhow. Not until I knew there was poaching going on.

Still, I realized an additional pair of ears and eyes would be useful. I decided to take my black lab, Mitzi, with me. I knew she'd alert me if she sensed danger.

I drove to the same spot the CI and I had parked, removed Mitzi's collar and we set off for Ian's woods. She was trained to walk no more than 20 feet in front of me. Once again, I carried only a sidearm and dressed in civilian clothes.

I stood on the hill above his house around 9 p.m. I stood there just long enough to note there were lights on inside and vehicles parked outside. I didn't hear music coming from inside the house. It was the middle of the week and everything seemed quiet.

Mitzi and I tramped 15 feet inside the tree line and slipped down the hill in an arc around the house, around the barn and out of sight.

My goal was to find the railroad line I'd heard about and follow it. The CI had said the trail led to deer feed Ian had planted. I wanted to see evidence of illegal hunting.

There could be shell casings, blood in the snow, signs one or more men had hauled out a carcass. Mitzi was trained to detect all of it. Even with snow, she would let me know if Ian or his friends had recently been busy.

I walked without using a flashlight, letting my eyes get used to the night and shadows.

It didn't take long for me to find the trail. It was elevated a few feet above the ground and ran perpendicular to the barn, set back about 160 feet from the main house.

I got up on it. Mitzi and I began walking. When I was certain we were out of sight of the house, and with the barn blocking me too, I bent low, cupped my hand over a small flashlight I'd tucked in my pocket and turned it on briefly to study the boot prints in the snow.

There were at least three different tread patterns. I couldn't tell if they were fresh and I didn't want to risk shining a light until I could figure it out. That tiny light could get me killed. I needed to keep moving and not risk anyone seeing me.

All along the trail, the trees branches had grown in, hiding it well. With several inches of snow on

the boughs, they bent lower, making it very hard
to see even 10 feet ahead.

If I made a mistake and Ian or one of his friends
found me on the property, it would be nearly
impossible to get away. And if Ian was hunting
tonight, he or a buddy would be carrying a
spotlight and one or more rifles.

Mitzi and I walked on slowly, stopping to listen,
then going further. I had to be careful not to
knock snow from branches above the trail.
That would be a sign to anyone following the
line that something tall had hit a bough.

One look down at the trail with a flashlight could
spell disaster.

Even if they didn't immediately notice my prints
were different than theirs, they would surely spot
Mitzi's paw prints. A closer inspection would
show a man and dog had walked the line together.

A child could track a man and his dog in this
snow. If we came face to face with Ian and one
of his buddies, or had to run for it, we'd be in
real trouble.

I pushed on another 50 feet when Mitzi suddenly
stopped. Her head went low. I froze and tried to
follow her gaze. But the dark and low branches

made it impossible to see.

A faint glow appeared 100 feet ahead, bouncing up and down, like someone walking and lazily holding a flashlight would do. Whoever it was, they were coming right for us.

Who? How many? I had no idea.

I only knew I had seconds to hide before we were discovered. Running was not an option. They'd hear us. I might end up with a bullet in my back.

I looked at both sides of the trail and when I spied a big fir tree with branches bent low into the trail, I took it. I signaled to Mitzi to come, took a big step and plunged off the trail and under the branches. I motioned for her to lie down and stay.

The light became brighter and I began to hear male voices.

I froze and Mitzi did too. I tried to make out how many men were coming our way.

I was hoping they were heatedly debating something like football, maybe what team would make it to the Super Bowl. I wanted them worked up about any topic, so they would focus on their discussion, not glance down and spot our tracks.

I had my hand on my holster, ready to draw my pistol if I had to. Mitzi didn't move a muscle.

I didn't want to think about what came next if I was discovered. I had to figure they were carrying guns. And with their friends back in the house less than 300 feet away, possibly multiple firearms there, and me with only a pistol and a dog, what kind of chance would we have in a gun battle?

I breathed as quietly as I could, kept my head down and put a hand up in front of Mitzi's eyes. I didn't want to take a chance on their beam reflecting her eyes.

The sound of boots shuffling through snow got louder. I listened for any change in their voices or in the lazy motion of the light. I prayed they would keep on tramping past us, then turn towards the house.

Closer. Closer. The alternating footfalls and the discussion told me there were two men walking towards us.

I saw the beam shine bright on the trail just a few feet from where we crouched in the tree well. One fellow was so close I could have reached out and grabbed his frozen, rawhide bootlace dragging in the snow.

Their voices stayed low and relaxed. The beam's angle jumped up and down like it was just a guide. They weren't really looking. They marched past us.

I stayed down and waited another minute. I was still concerned they might notice my fresh tracks or Mitzi's paw prints. If they did, there'd be a firestorm of action.

When I saw the light leave the trail and point towards the house, I took a deep breath and patted Mitzi. And I decided I didn't want to push my luck any further that night.

I'd have liked to hike the entire trail Ian had set up, look for more evidence of night hunting. But it was just too risky.

Still, I'd seen enough to tell me Ian and a pal were indeed hunting at night and using the old rail line to do it, just as the CI had told me years earlier.

When I was confident the men were far enough away they could not hear us, Mitzi and I crawled out from under the back side of the big fir. We hiked quietly up the hill, away from Ian's, back to my car.

I hadn't seen any guns, only a light shining and heard two men talking. But common sense told me whoever they were, they were hunting deer.

As I drove home with Mitzi sleeping off our close call in the back seat, I began working on a plan to stop the poaching once and for all.

And the next day, when I had it set in my mind what I wanted to do, I asked my wife if she could spare a couple of bed sheets. I said they didn't have to be new, old would do fine. But they needed to be all white, nothing with a design on them. Big enough to cover a man, but not so big he'd get tripped up.

Her eyebrows went up. She always knew when I was up to something.

"Halloween's over, John," she laughed, teasing me a bit.

"I know," I said with a chuckle. "But I've got a good reason. Just don't ask me what it is right now, okay? And could you help me for a few minutes? We'll need sharp scissors."

She told me to look in the sewing basket for them while she went to a closet to find the sheets. We met up at the kitchen table. It was time for some sheet surgery.

"Now what?" she asked.

"I'm going to drop a sheet over my head. I want you to make sure I'm totally covered, front and back and sides, and then I need for you to cut holes for my eyes and a smaller hole for a mouth – just so a fellow could breathe," I explained.

She paused with the scissors in her hand and asked, "I'm not going to be getting these sheets back, am I?"

I shook my head and admitted, "Probably not. I don't think you'd want them anyway. You'd have to patch them."

She sighed before cutting the first eyehole, laughed and said, "Oh well. It's probably time for some new sheets anyhow."

Once the holes were in place, I folded the sheets up, one at a time, and tucked them in a duffle bag.

Now, it was time to put my team together.

Deputy Warden Marc Luneau insisted on being part of it. By now, he'd been on the job awhile. I knew I could count on him. And I had a warden trainee with me, Robert Rooks. He wanted in too.

Warden Roger Whitcomb agreed to serve as back up, listening in case we got into trouble. He and his deputies would set up in an abandoned building, not far from Ian's.

If they heard we were in trouble, they'd come running to assist and call in even more troops, if necessary. Gonyaw was out of state or he most certainly would have been a part of it too.

They all knew how dangerous Ian was. And, just in case they didn't take me seriously, I reminded them of Ian's courtroom statements, before he went off to prison a few years earlier.

Ian testified under oath – in front of the judge, in front of his own defense attorney who grimaced when he heard his client speak – that he had shot up into the woods not for fun, but to kill me.

"Yes, I meant to kill him," he told the court while he glared at me from the witness stand. "I'm only sorry I missed."

Just out of prison and back to night hunting, I doubted Ian's feelings about me had changed any. If anything, Ian would be more wary, more intent on killing me and any other law officer who came onto his land.

My plan was to ambush him.

I wanted a night with a partial moon to provide light for us. We couldn't risk shining flashlights.

I also wanted fresh snow so we could easily spot new tracks along the rail bed. In a few days, we had both.

Still, it was a big gamble. Ian knew the ledges, the shortcuts and hiding places on his 200 acres. I'd only walked a small portion of his land. Had I seen enough?

And what about his friends inside the farmhouse? If they heard something going on – or if Ian called out for help – would they come charging out to help him? What firepower would they bring? Had they purchased more automatic weapons? Would they use them?

The plan was for me to walk the trail in uniform with Rooks and Luneau hidden behind me, each covered in a sheet. They would carry sidearms only, stick to the sides of the trail, hiding beneath the tree boughs, lying in the snow if they had to.

I didn't want Ian to know they were even there.

Some guys give up when they see a lot of law enforcement coming at them. But other fellows, it seems to push them over the edge. They feel overwhelmed and make bad choices.

Around 8 p.m., Luneau and Rooks and I headed to Ian's to watch the house briefly, before dropping down to the rail line.

Lights were on inside. Shadows crossed in front of the windows now and again, telling us people were home. It seemed a TV was on, as I could see flickering colors too.

We waited until we saw the front door open. Two people headed out into the night. When they had disappeared into the far side of the woods, we assumed the pair would follow the trail like the CI had told me years before.

We stood still another 10 minutes. Then I sent Rooks and Luneau down the ridge, to set up along the rail bed.

I gave them time to hide. Then I marched on down the hill as quietly as I could, hidden inside the woods, but in full uniform this time, a shotgun in my arms.

It was loaded with law enforcement caliber buckshot – strong enough to kill a man, maybe two or even three at close range. There were nine pellets in each shell and those pellets spread. And on my hip, I wore my revolver.

I knew Ian would be carrying a rifle, maybe a handgun as well. Anyone with him might have firearms too, even if they were just shining the light for him.

I didn't want to think about what would happen
if Ian saw me before I saw him. This was his
land. I'd only been up a little section of the trail.
I wondered how angry he was. If he still wanted me
dead, how far would he go to make that happen?

I was counting on the element of surprise.
I hoped it would be enough.

We figured the hunters would walk the route and
come into our trap in an hour or less, like the CI
had told me.

But an hour went by and then another 30
minutes. There was still no sign of them.
Rooks and Luneau were lying in the snow waiting.
I was in front of them 25 feet or so, standing
quietly, hidden by snow bent branches, poised
to pounce.

The waiting began to take a toll. Where were
they? What was the hold up?

Did they suspect something? Were they onto us?
Had they left the rail bed? Were they above us on
the ridge? What had changed?

I was concerned and was certain Rooks and
Luneau were too. But none of us moved. And we

certainly did not talk. Each of us held his position, listened and waited.

Another 10 minutes went by. I was beginning to think we should abort the mission. Something was seriously wrong.

BAM!

A single rifle shot sounded not more than 20 yards up the trail.

My mind raced to pinpoint the exact location and the caliber of the shot. It was a deer rifle, for sure. Had Ian shot at a deer? I stood and listened for a second shot. My deputies would not move until they got a signal from me.

I stepped out from the shadows and began running up the center of the trail, towards the shot. The snow on the tree limbs was so heavy, it was like running through a tunnel of snow and shadows, even with the moonlight.

Rooks and Luneau leaped out of their snowy beds and ran behind me, staying back 25 feet. They darted beneath the tree boughs, in and out of the shadows.

I rounded a bend. I had to be getting close to the shooter. Where was he?

A figure stepped out of the trees and onto the trail. He'd heard me coming. He stood glowering at me, 20 feet away. Beside him stood a smaller man.

I knew immediately, just from the way the figure stood – feet spread wide, back ramrod straight, chin up, blocking my way forward – it was Ian.

He had a rifle slung over his shoulder and a large revolver on his hip. His hand went for the pistol as soon as he saw my uniform.

"Ian! Put the gun down. NOW! Or you'll die here tonight," I shouted to him.

My shotgun was pointed at his chest, safety off, my finger on the trigger with pressure applied. The slightest twitch of my index finger and my gun would fire.

I waited to see if he would do what he was told. If he lifted that pistol just a fraction more, there would be blood in the snow.

Whoever was standing there beside him, they would be badly hurt too, maybe even killed.

I couldn't think about that. I had tunnel vision. My eyes were on Ian and his left hand. If he didn't drop the pistol, if he raised it up just an inch more, I would have to shoot.

IAN

I knew Ian had probably laid in his prison bed
and dreamed of killing me.

"Put the gun back in the holster, Ian!"
I commanded him again. "Now!"

As Ian stood there thinking, I knew Rooks and
Luneau each had their revolvers trained on Ian's
chest, even if he didn't know they were there.

If Ian was really fast or lucky, he might shoot me
once. But it wasn't likely with my trigger finger so
close to firing the shotgun. And in a gun battle
with three wardens? He wouldn't walk away.

Ian was no dummy. He knew being caught with
firearms meant he was headed back to prison.
And if he'd hit a deer with that shot we heard a few
minutes earlier, we'd have him for poaching too.

The guy standing beside Ian – all bundled up
so I couldn't see his face – his shoulders began
to shake.

"Last time, Ian. Take your hand off the pistol.
Then raise both your hands slowly over your
head," I told him.

Ian's shoulders rounded, his chin dropped a bit.
He took his hand off the revolver. The gun rested
again in its holster.

I took my finger off the trigger and lowered the shotgun's muzzle as Luneau and Rooks rushed in to handcuff Ian and the second man.

When Rooks pulled back the hood on the guy next to Ian, the three of us quietly gasped.

It was a teenage girl beneath the parka's hood. The heavy winter coat, mittens and boots had hid her gender. Tears were streaming down her face.

Ian stood, jaw set, eyes straight ahead, unbowed, ignoring her. He hadn't said a word.

But his tough guy demeanor changed when a voice was heard on the hillside, crying, "Dad? Don't shoot! Don't shoot! It's me! Dad, where are you? Don't shoot!"

He came alive. "Maggie?" he cried out. "Maggie? What are you doing here?"

A second girl hiked towards us through the snow. We followed her flashlight beam as it sifted through the snowy boughs. A teenaged girl – unarmed and alone – stepped onto the trail, crying so hard she barely made any sense.

"Dad, your bullet hit the tree right next to me," the daughter said between choking gasps and tears. She ran to him until we stopped and held her, just 10 feet from Ian. "You almost killed me!"

Ian struggled to get the cuffs off. "Maggie! Maggie! Oh my God! I'm sorry! I didn't know! I didn't know it was you! I thought you were Kapusta! Oh my God! Are you all right? Maggie! Maggie! Let me go! Let me go," he shouted.

"I went looking for you because you and Debbie were gone so long," she said. "I was afraid something had happened, that you were hurt."

"I told you to stay in the house!" he said, raising his voice. Then he felt bad for shouting at her and added, "I'm sorry, Maggie. I didn't know it was you."

Now we had three people – Ian and two teenage girls – and they were all in shock, realizing how close they each had come to dying just a few minutes earlier.

And it wasn't lost on Rooks, Luneau or me how close we had come to a deadly shoot out either.

The three of us marched Ian and the girls towards the house. Whitcomb was informed by radio we had Ian in custody and came down and met us.

Before the night was over, we learned why that particular night hunt was different. Ian's buddies were away. His daughter was visiting and she had invited a friend for a sleepover.

Ian had offered to show his daughter's friend how he hunted at night and she had agreed to tag along. When Ian's daughter worried they had been gone too long, she picked up a flashlight and went looking for the pair.

When things calmed down, it was back to jail again for Ian.

He was charged by the state with reckless endangerment for shooting into the night at a human being. The next day, the ATF stepped in again as well.

Funny thing was, I still could not charge Ian with attempting to poach deer. I hadn't even seen him shine a light. There was no dead or wounded deer. Ian's target was me.

This time, he got three years in federal prison. And once again, things went quiet over at his place while he was behind bars. At least, I didn't get any complaints. But it didn't end there. Imagine my surprise, when, on a cold, dark November night several years later, the phone rang and the caller was Ian.

"My neighbor's dogs are coming onto my property

and running deer. I don't like it. I want you to take care of it," he said. "You do that, right?"

"Yes, Ian," I said, same as if I was talking to anyone else who called with a complaint. "We deal with dogs chasing deer. What's the owner's name?"

He told me and I recognized the fellow. He was no saint either. I'd had to talk with him a time or two before about his hunting practices.

But listening to Ian tell me how he was upset with his neighbor, I was of two minds.

The first little voice told me, "Ian may have a legitimate complaint." But the fellow who recalled almost having his head shot off argued, "This could be Ian's way of getting you over to his place. He might be about to follow through on what he's wanted to do for a long time – kill you."

Both arguments were valid. Which was it?

There was no way to know.

"One more thing. I'd like you to come to my house tonight," Ian said. "Will you do that?"

Well, here's a guy who wanted me to leave him alone, who has shot to kill me to make certain

I stayed away. Now, he wants me to drop by for a visit?

Strange.

Still, I didn't want him thinking I was afraid of him. I wasn't. But that didn't mean I was a fool either.

So, I said, "Yes, I can do that, Ian. I'll be by in a few hours," and I hung up the phone and stared at it for a few seconds, shaking my head and wondering, "What's he up to now?"

I let my wife know where I was headed and told her if she didn't hear from me by midnight, to let my neighboring wardens know.

She looked at me like I'd just said I was going skydiving at night without a parachute.

"John, if you insist on going over there, at least take someone with you," she said. "Please, don't go there alone."

"Ahh, don't worry. I'll be all right," I said. "Just call the fellows if you don't hear from me in a few hours."

She shook her head, but didn't argue. She knew it was hopeless trying to tell me what to do.

IAN

I drove over to Ian's and again saw Rhode Island
license plates on vehicles parked in the driveway.
Was it a coincidence he had those guests here, I
wondered? Or were they part of another plan to
kill me?

I got out of my cruiser and walked to the door
with my sidearm on my hip.

I knocked on his front door. Ian opened it wide,
nodded and ushered me inside.

"Come on in. Come on in," he said. He didn't
smile exactly, but he was a lot more civil to me
than he had ever been before. Once I stepped
inside, he shut the door behind me.

I immediately noticed four other fellows seated
in front of a television in an adjoining room, off
to my left. It looked like their attention was on a
basketball game. I caught two of them glancing
at me over their shoulders, but they didn't appear
overly concerned and no one got up.

"Thanks for coming," Ian said. "My neighbor's
got two big dogs. He lets them loose at night and
they're coming over onto my property and chasing
deer," he told me. "I know that's not right. I want
you to stop it."

"Can you describe the dogs for me? Are they

wearing collars?" I asked him.

Ian said the dogs were Rottweilers. He hadn't paid attention to their collars.

"How about some dates and times when you've seen them on your land?" I asked him.

"Sure," he said and he went off to look at a calendar hanging on the wall and began reciting dates and times and exactly where on his land he saw the dogs.

"You can see their tracks coming from his place to mine through the woods," he added.

I listened, scratched down a few notes, nodded and told him I would visit his neighbor and tell him to keep his dogs at home.

"If you see the dogs over here again, let me know. I'll take it further," I told him. And with that, I shut my notebook and tucked my pen back in my breast pocket.

"All right, Ian," I said, winding up my visit, "I'll be off."

I turned sideways to head back to the front door.

"Hey, uh, just a second," he said to me. "I've got

---

something I want to you to see."

I turned back to face him. "What's that?" I asked.

"It's down in the basement. You'll have to go down there to see it."

He was looking into my face – the picture of innocence – waiting for me to blink, to flinch, to make any kind of excuse to get out of going down into the old farmhouse cellar with him.

He knew I knew I'd be trapped down there.

Does he want to kill me or just scare me? What could be in the cellar that he couldn't just bring upstairs and show me?

I knew his buddies were listening even if their heads were pointed at the television. They were part of whatever plan Ian had for me.

If I went down into that basement I'd be closer to being in real trouble if Ian and his pals were planning to kill me. This old home didn't even have an entry into the cellar from the outside like modern houses. It would be five against one and only one way out.

Yell for help? No homes within a half mile. No one would hear a thing.

I kept my poker face and behaved like going down into the cellar with a guy whose goal it had been to murder me for going on a decade now – his house staffed with cronies of the same caliber – was no big deal.

"Okay, Ian. I guess I can spare a minute," I told him. "You lead the way."

I was not so crazy I would go first and have him follow me. I wanted just a little advantage, in case his plan was to stick a knife or gun in my back or club me over the head.

Ian nodded, grinned, turned and led me to an old painted wooden door near the kitchen. He opened it, reached over and pulled a string that turned on a single bulb.

It shone dimly over worn wooden stairs.

When he placed a foot on the first tread, I reached for my holster and popped the keeper free.

That would make it easier for me to pull my revolver if I needed it.

If he planned to turn on me or had buddies down there waiting to jump me, I wanted to be ready. Every fraction of a second counts when you have to defend yourself.

He trotted nimbly down the stairs and I followed at a slower pace. I wanted my eyes to adjust to the dim light and look around the room while I was descending. I let him get a few arm lengths in front of me.

When I met him at the bottom of the stairs, he turned to face me and grinned.

He took two steps towards a workbench covered with tools, pulled another light chain and lit up a small woodworking shop.

"I want you to see this," he said. "Yer gonna love it."

He reached up and opened a cupboard door above the workbench and pulled out a sawed off shotgun he had hidden there. The business part of the weapon was pointed away from us.

"Check out the stock on this baby," he grinned. "I carved it myself."

The subject matter was not something you would show to polite company. It might make some fellows chuckle, but that was about it. Still, it was clear Ian was proud of his work.

"It's walnut. Choice stuff," he said running his hand along the stock.

I said the nicest thing I could think of, "That must have taken a lot of work, Ian."

"Oh yeah. Hours," he said, as if it was a grand piano. "Lots and lots of hours." He smiled like a teenager who had just purchased his first car. It was the happiest I'd ever seen the man.

I nodded. I was wondering again why in the world Ian was still playing with guns and even nuttier, showing me a gun.

I listened for the sound of someone creeping up on me or the sight of shadows shifting.

"I bet nobody has a shotgun stock like this," Ian said proudly.

"You probably right," I told him, then changed the subject.

"I've got another appointment, Ian. I need to get going," I said to hurry him along.

"Oh. Yeah. Sure," he said. He turned back to the work counter, tucked the shotgun back into the cabinet, shut the door and smiled at me.

"After you," I said, stepping back and letting him lead the way upstairs.

He got it.

"Yeah, well, I just wanted you to see that," he said.

"No problem," I said.

He exited into the main house and I paused a little at the top of the stairs just for a split second to count heads again. The same number of guys were looking at the TV. None of them had moved. I didn't hear anyone coming up behind me.

I followed Ian to the front door and said, "All right then, Ian. I'll speak with your neighbor about his dogs. I hope that solves your problem. If it doesn't, you let me know."

He nodded and I opened the front door and left his home. I walked to my cruiser and drove off wondering what all this had been about.

Getting me to come to his home at night? Asking me to go down into the cellar? Showing me the shotgun? It was all some sort of test, I was certain.

I took a deep breath, shook my head and headed down the road and pulled into the driveway of Ian's neighbor. The dogs Ian was complaining about ran up to greet me. There were tracks everywhere. It was clear he was telling the truth about the dogs running free at night.

I talked to the owner, gave him a written warning and urged him to keep his dogs home. Dogs chasing deer was a serious problem. He said he would fence them in.

And for a long time afterwards, things were quiet over in that part of my district. I didn't get complaints about Ian or complaints from him.

About three years later, I was at a gun show in Barre, staffing a booth for the Department. The annual event was always busy, with hundreds of guys, and women too, crowding the aisles. Some people go to buy guns, some want to sell. Many just want to look and chat with collectors or shooting sports enthusiasts.

There were two of us manning the booth. We were there to answer questions about hunting and firearms, hand out copies of Vermont's regulations and a few freebies.

My partner for the day had gone off to get some coffee, when out of the corner of my eye, I saw a familiar cap weaving back and forth in the mob of men headed my way, 80 feet away.

I recognized the headgear immediately as Ian's. He liked to wear a Scottish tam when he was out in public. There might not be a lot of people who could do that without getting some ribbing outside of Scotland or some festival, but Ian could.

Anyone who might dare make a wise remark would likely risk a broken nose. He was very proud of his Scottish heritage. Whenever he wore the tam, he walked with an even bigger swagger.

A convicted felon who had served two additional sentences for possession of firearms attending Vermont's biggest gun show? It was like a fellow with a permanently suspended driver's license attending a car auction with money enough to buy one or two.

"Why would a guy even do this to himself?" I wondered.

I was concerned that when Ian saw me in uniform, with the big "Vermont Fish and Wildlife" banner hanging behind me, the sight of me might rile him.

I wasn't responsible for him committing the crimes that got him banned for life from being around guns. But my reporting him for ignoring that ban had certainly cost him in recent years.

How many years had he spent in prison now because he just wouldn't leave them alone? Five or more years, was it?

I didn't want anything unpleasant to occur at

this event. It was designed to be a good time for everyone who enjoyed firearms, their history and the workmanship that goes into making them.

I didn't want any part in possibly giving the show a black eye.

I stood on my tiptoes, trying to see over and into the crowd in front of my table. I was looking for my partner, to see if he was on his way back yet. Maybe he had stopped to talk to someone at a nearby booth?

If I found him, I could duck out for a bit before Ian got carried along in the sea of humanity and plunked down right in front of me. But my partner was nowhere to be seen.

The throng – three and four abreast – kept creeping closer and closer. I was as uncomfortable as a reluctant groom standing at the altar hearing the organist strike up the Wedding March.

The aisles were jammed. There was nowhere to go. Whenever a fellow stopped at a booth somewhere ahead to talk to somebody about a weapon or a display, the whole line ground to a halt like a Manhattan traffic jam.

I smiled, talked briefly to a father and son. I handed them some literature as they were jostled by fellows behind them. We smiled and agreed it was certainly a big crowd this year. But out of the corner of my eye, I saw the tam coming closer. It reminded me of a shark smelling blood in the water.

Ian had been on the other side of the throng when I first spied his distinctive cap. He had drifted closer to my side of the aisle as the gap between us closed. I knew he had seen me. He would have had to do that on purpose.

He was coming for me. I pretended I didn't notice.

In another 20 seconds, Ian and I came face to face. The only thing separating us was the pressed board table, maybe two feet wide.

He stopped in his tracks and said loudly, "Kapusta!" stood up straight and pretended he was surprised to see me standing there in front of him.

The fellows behind Ian didn't bump into him. They all made a point of giving him space. It was like they knew he was dangerous.

I stood. Waited. I didn't say a word.

Ian's eyes narrowed and his smile disappeared. He bent at the waist and leaned in over the table,

closer to me. He made a fist with his left hand
and rapped his knuckles on the table so hard
the papers jumped an inch. Then he leaned in
closer to me, and pointed at my chest – just three
inches away.

Ian looked me in the eye and said, "I've got a lot of
respect for you."

He nodded slightly, smiled a crooked smile,
straightened his back, turned and pushed
through the crowd like Moses parting the Red Sea
and disappeared.

And that was the last I ever saw of Ian McLeod.
He died in a work accident the following Spring.

He'd worked dangerous construction jobs to
pay the bills. I was told Ian would take on jobs
few men had the guts to tackle – standing on
scaffolding hundreds of feet up in the air
– buffeted by wind and cold. He was good at it and
earned big money working all over the East Coast.

When I got word Ian was dead, I felt kinda
funny. Not like I'd lost a friend exactly, but like
I'd definitely lost something.

What was it?

If he'd gone back to poaching, I wouldn't have

hesitated to go after him again. He knew that. And I suspect he would have been just as willing to take another shot at my head if I tried to stop him again.

After nearly a decade, neither one of us had changed sides.

And after thinking about it, it finally struck me why I felt a kind of loss at the news of Ian's death.

I realized we're all used to having a friend, a spouse, a family member or a boss tell us, "Good job," now and again.

But when a fellow who has spent years wanting you dead – who tried to kill you several times – when that man tells you he respects you?

Well, maybe it's a funny thing to say, but Mr. McLeod's words meant a lot to me.

Acknowledgements

This book could not have been completed without the encouragement and skill of the following individuals:

Jean McHenry
Sam Stanley
Dorrice Hammer
Inge Schaefer
Sandra Brisson
Joel Higginbotham
Jean Cross
Paul Young
Rhonda Hanley
Stephen Frost
Debra Russell Sanborn
O.C.
and
Muffaluffagus

Thank you, one and all.

MANY THANKS TO THE FOLLOWING FOR ALLOWING ME TO SHARE THEIR STORIES

 **Denny Gaiotti** worked 29 years as a Vermont warden. Denny lived in Whiting, VT.

 **John Kapusta** worked 38 years as a Vermont warden. John resides in Hardwick.

 **Walt Ackermann** worked 19 years as a deputy warden. Walt resides in Cabot.

 **Ken Denton** worked 30 years as a Vermont warden. Ken resides in Cabot.

Stories By Warden

Denny Gaiotti

Buoy Blab

How's the Fishing?

Stinkers

John Kapusta

Deputy's First Day

Willoughby Baptism

Rocky Rescue

Don't Be Late

Ian

Walt Ackermann

Snack Attack

Ken Denton

Concord Chase

Gimmee the Keys

Who We Are

 **Megan Price** is a former award winning journalist and Vermont legislator. She enjoys turning good stories into great reading.

 **Carrie Cook** is an exceptional graphic designer and bass player who lives in Cambridge.

 **Bob Lutz** is a talented caricaturist, and former warden. Bob lives in Fairfax.

 **Tyler Denis** is a web and graphic designer who lives in Williamstown.

Want more great warden stories?